A very uncivil war

Famous

People & Events

in the

War Between the States

A Skill-Based Reading Anthology

Editorial Director: Susan C. Thies
Editor: Paula J. Reece
Contributing Writer: Julie Cahalan
Book Design: Jann Williams
Production: Mark Hagenberg
Photo Research: Lisa Lorimor

Image Credits
Digital Stock: pp. 17, 34, 36, 84–85, 95, 103. Dover: 18, 56, 73, 74, 87, 110.
Library of Congress: cover, pp. 6–7, 8, 11, 26, 28, 46–47, 48, 50, 65, 67, 101, 109.
National Archives: pp. 4, 86. www.arttoday.com: pp. 59, 93.

For information, contact
Perfection Learning® Corporation
1000 North Second Avenue, P.O. Box 500
Logan, Iowa 51546-0500.
Phone: 800-831-4190 • Fax: 712-644-2392
perfectionlearning.com

ISBN 0-7891-5584-2
Printed in the U.S.A.

contents

helping those
in need

Harriet Tubman

Conductor of Freedom

by Shirley Jordan

Harriet Tubman was born around 1820. She lived in a crude cabin with a dirt floor and no windows. She was a nobody—a slave child.

²By the time she was six years old, she was a servant in her master's house. Her jobs were to help peel potatoes and carry water from the well. She scrubbed the floors on her hands and knees. And she had to keep the master's baby happy, even though it was all she could do to lift him.

³As a slave, Harriet had no rights. Her master or mistress could work her from sunrise to sunset. They could whip her as they wished. If their baby cried, she was whipped.

⁴"I've told you and told you," her mistress panted between blows of the leather strap. "Never let the baby cry."

⁵"But, Missus. I couldn't make him stop."

⁶Again, the whip lashed across her back.

⁷"And what else have I told you?" her mistress yelled. "Don't talk back!"

⁸Harriet's parents, brothers, and sisters were all slaves on a tobacco plantation near the village of Bucktown, Maryland. Life was bad. There was always the fear of being sold down South to the cotton planters.

⁹Sometimes Ma would try to console her children. She'd say, "We got it good alongside those cotton slaves down South."

¹⁰Harriet wasn't very old when she learned that the South was bad. The North was good. Old Ned had said so, and he ought to know.

¹¹Old Ned had been born on the slave ship that brought his people from Africa to America. He was the oldest person on the plantation.

[12]"Up North, a Negro can be free," he said. "Nobody can own slaves."

[13]He told all the other slaves Bible stories and taught them songs. Harriet learned about the children of Israel who had been held in Egypt by the Pharaoh. She'd raise her voice and sing loudly the songs Old Ned taught.

[14]*Go down, Moses,*

Way down in Egypt's land.

Tell ol' Pharaoh,

Let my people go.

[15]One night, two slaves disappeared from a neighboring plantation. It was then that Harriet first learned about the Underground Railroad.

[16]"It's not a real train," Old Ned explained. "Its conductors are people who are against slavery. They hide slaves in their homes. When it is safe, the slaves move to the next station. They finally get North to the free states. There they find jobs and homes."

[17]From then on, Harriet could think of nothing else. One day she would go North and be free.

[18]Harriet was 15. She was sent to a country store on an errand. An overseer from a plantation nearby came in with a slave.

[19]"You wait in the corner, Jim," the overseer said. "Soon as I get this order filled, you can tote it home."

[20]Suddenly, Jim bolted for the open door.

[21]"Get back here, you black devil!" roared the overseer. He looked at Harriet and cried, "Grab him, girl! Grab him."

[22]But Harriet jumped in front of the white man. She stretched out her arms. Over her shoulders, she could see Jim running into the woods.

[23]In a rage, the overseer grabbed a heavy weight off the counter. He threw it at Harriet. It hit her on the side of the head.

[24]For a long time after that, Harriet was unconscious. She was not expected to live. For the rest of her life, she had a deep dent in her head. She suffered from sleeping spells. She could fall asleep while hoeing in the field or carrying a bucket of water from the well.

[25]Harriet was 24 years old when she married John Tubman, a free Negro. John was quite content with his life. He tried to discourage Harriet when she talked of riding the Underground Railroad to freedom.

[26]It didn't bother John that he was not allowed to own land, vote,

carry a gun, attend a church that had a black minister, or even own a dog. He just liked being called "free."

[27]The time came for Harriet to run away. She kept it a secret from her husband.

[28]Harriet had heard about the white people who were called Quakers. She knew that they hated slavery. They even helped Negroes escape up North.

[29]It was through a Quaker family who lived in Bucktown that Harriet got the information she needed. They told her the route to freedom.

[30]"Just follow the Choptank River. Go to where it begins at the border between Maryland and Delaware. Then take the road to Camden. Go northeast until you come to a clapboard house with green shutters."

[31]Harriet's brothers, William, Robert, and Benjamin, set out with her. But in a short time, they decided the risks were too great.

[32]"We'll never make it, sister," said William. "They'll catch us. Things will be worse than ever."

[33]Benjamin pleaded, "Come back with us. Please."

[34]But Harriet went on alone. For two weeks, she trudged through woods, meadows, and thickets.

Sometimes she waded in water and mud.

[35]Most of the time, she traveled at night. But she kept going. Often she sang silently, "I'm bound for the promised land."

[36]At last the door of the clapboard house opened. A kind voice said, "Come in, friend. Thee are welcome." Harriet breathed a sigh of joy.

[37]But Harriet was not completely satisfied—not when so many of her family and friends were still in bondage. And as wonderful as it was to be free, Harriet was lonely. She had to go back to set them free.

[38]Harriet began her life as "Moses."

[39]She crossed into enemy territory 19 times. She succeeded in leading more than 300 slaves to freedom. The reward for her capture eventually reached $40,000. In spite of the danger, she never gave up.

[40]The slave owners were furious. "Something must be done about that thieving black wench," they ranted. "She ought to be strung up."

[41]In 1850, the Fugitive Slave Law was passed. Slaves were no longer safe in any of the states. The new law denied runaway slaves the right to a trial if caught. Anyone

found aiding a slave could be fined and imprisoned.

[42]There were nearly 50,000 Negroes living in the North at the time. Most of them were escaped slaves.

[43]Once more, they had to flee to freedom. This time they went to Canada where they were welcome.

[44]The new law made Harriet's job a little more difficult. The Underground Railroad would have to run a little farther north. But it would not stop.

[45]Harriet's fame grew. She was talked about in every town from Canada to the Gulf of Mexico.

[46]"What a daring woman," they said. "She must have magical powers!"

[47]"She's another Moses," some stated. "She's freeing her people single-handed."

[48]Blacks claimed she was ten feet tall! She could see in the dark! She could jump over rivers and mountains too.

[49]Harriet Tubman laughed at these claims. But she did say, "As a conductor of the Underground Railroad, I can say what most conductors can't. I never ran my train off the track. And I never lost a passenger."

Thousands of slaves, such as these in Virginia, ran away to freedom during the Civil War.

[50]When the Civil War began in 1861, Harriet volunteered as a nurse, cook, and laundress to help the Union. She and other volunteer escaped slaves followed the army from camp to camp.

[51]At the request of General Hunter, Harriet formed a group of scouts to go ahead of the troops. They looked for rebel outposts.

[52]"It's very dangerous, Harriet," the general said. "I'll understand if you refuse."

[53]"I was born to danger, sir," Harriet replied.

[54]Because of Harriet and her black scouts, many successful raids were made.

[55]Harriet had discovered one of the main Confederate camps at Green Pond. It was not far from the Combahee River. There were big plantations with hundreds of slaves on both sides of the river.

[56]"We should surprise them in the middle of the night," Harriet explained to Colonel James Montgomery. "Then we could wipe out their supplies."

[57]"But we'd have to take boats up the river in the dark," the colonel reasoned. "We don't know the river. There are sure to be torpedoes in the water. It's not safe."

[58]"My scouts know the river. And we know where the explosives are. We can steer around them easily."

[59]At last, Colonel Montgomery was convinced. He put Harriet in charge of 300 black soldiers.

[60]Three Union gunboats left St. Helena Sound at midnight. The mission was a big success. They captured the Confederate camp and destroyed the supplies. They also freed 800 slaves from plantations and took them back to the army base.

[61]After the war, Harriet returned to Auburn, New York. There she cared for her aged parents and continued working for her people.

[62]In 1869, Sarah Hopkins Bradford wrote a biography of Harriet, *Scenes in the Life of Harriet Tubman*. Harriet received $1,200 of the proceeds. She used that and her government pension money to manage an old folks' home for Negroes. She called it the John Brown Home.

[63]She continued working for her people until she died on March 10, 1913. She was given a military funeral.

[64]In 1914, a bronze plaque in her memory was hung on the wall of the Cayuga County New York Courthouse.

If you have been timing your reading speed for this story, record your time below.

_____ : _____

Minutes   **Seconds**

UNDERSTANDING THE MAIN IDEA

The following questions will demonstrate your understanding of what the story is about, or the *main idea*. Choose the best answer for each question.

1. This story is mainly about

Ⓐ daily slave life in the South.

Ⓑ Harriet Tubman's life and work.

Ⓒ how to run a plantation.

Ⓓ the punishments slaves received.

2. This story could have been titled

Ⓐ "Don't Talk Back!"

Ⓑ "Moses and the Pharaoh."

Ⓒ "Bound for the Promised Land."

Ⓓ "Kitchen Slaves."

3. Which detail best supports the main idea of this story?

Ⓐ Harriet often sang silently, "I'm bound for the promised land."

Ⓑ One night, two slaves disappeared from a neighboring plantation.

Ⓒ Harriet scrubbed the floors on her hands and knees.

Ⓓ In 1850, the Fugitive Slave Law was passed.

4. Find another detail that supports the main idea of this story. Write it on the lines below.

_____

_____

_____

_____

RECALLING FACTS

The following questions will test how well you remember the facts in the story you just read. Choose the best answer for each question.

1. Harriet Tubman and her family were

Ⓐ slaves on a cotton plantation in Alabama.

Ⓑ shipped to America from Africa.

Ⓒ all slaves in their master's house.

Ⓓ slaves in Maryland.

2. When she was 15, Harriet Tubman

Ⓐ ran away to the North.

Ⓑ was hit in the head with a heavy weight.

Ⓒ caught an escaping slave in a country store.

Ⓓ learned how to read and write.

3. Harriet Tubman escaped slavery

Ⓐ on a barge in the Mississippi River.

Ⓑ when Union soldiers set her free during the Civil War.

Ⓒ on the Underground Railroad.

Ⓓ because her mother took her to the North.

4. During her years as a conductor on the Underground Railroad, Harriet Tubman

Ⓐ never lost a passenger.

Ⓑ was occasionally caught but always escaped again.

Ⓒ helped slaves return to Africa.

Ⓓ once ran the train off the track.

READING BETWEEN THE LINES

An *inference* is a conclusion drawn from facts. A *generalization* is a general statement, idea, or rule that is supported by facts. Analyze the story by choosing the best answer to each question below.

1. What conclusion can you draw from paragraphs 12–14?

Ⓐ Slaves did not practice Christianity.

Ⓑ Slaves compared themselves to Israelites in Bible stories.

Ⓒ Plantation owners allowed slaves to have Sundays off to attend church services.

Ⓓ Old Ned had been a choir teacher in Africa before he was forced into slavery.

2. What conclusion can you draw from paragraphs 25–27?

Ⓐ Harriet was forced to marry John Tubman, a free Negro.

Ⓑ There were many free Negroes in Maryland when Harriet was growing up.

Ⓒ Free Negroes had the same rights as other U.S. citizens.

Ⓓ Some free Negroes weren't really all that free compared to whites.

3. What generalization can you make from this story?

Ⓐ Some people wanted all slaves to be free.

Ⓑ Slave overseers were generally very kind and gentle with slaves.

Ⓒ It was easy for slaves to escape on the Underground Railroad.

Ⓓ All Union soldiers were afraid to attack in the night.

4. It can be inferred from the story that the Union army

Ⓐ didn't really want to help escaped slaves start a new life.

Ⓑ paid Harriet well to be a scout and spy.

Ⓒ thought Harriet would be a good scout.

Ⓓ used only escaped slaves as scouts.

—■—

A Very UnCivil War

DETERMINING CAUSE AND EFFECT

Choose the best answers for the following questions to show the relationship between what happened in the story (*effects*) and why those things happened (*causes*).

1. Because Harriet Tubman was a slave,

Ⓐ her master had to feed and clothe her well.

Ⓑ she had no rights.

Ⓒ she married a free Negro.

Ⓓ her brothers and sisters were slaves.

2. What happened because two slaves escaped from a nearby plantation?

Ⓐ Harriet learned about the Underground Railroad.

Ⓑ Old Ned tried to escape.

Ⓒ The slaves were caught and returned to their owner.

Ⓓ Harriet's brothers decided to try to escape.

3. Why did Harriet Tubman have to take escaping slaves to Canada after 1850?

Ⓐ There was no more room in the northern states for escaping slaves.

Ⓑ No one in the United States would hire an escaped slave.

Ⓒ The Fugitive Slave Law made it harder for escaped slaves to remain free.

Ⓓ Escaped slaves were afraid the Union army would force them to fight in the Civil War.

4. Why did Harriet Tubman keep her decision to run away a secret from her husband?

_____

_____

_____

_____

_____

_____

_____

_____

_____

_____

_____

_____

_____

_____

_____

_____

_____

_____

_____

_____

_____

_____

_____

_____

_____

_____

_____

_____

USING CONTEXT CLUES

Skilled readers can often find the meaning of unfamiliar words by using *context clues*. This means they study the way the words are used in the text.

Use the context clues in the excerpts below to determine the meaning of each **bold-faced** word. Then choose the answer that best matches the meaning of the word.

1. "[Harriet] lived in a **crude** cabin with a dirt floor and no windows."

CLUE: "She was a nobody—a slave child. . . . Life was bad."

Ⓐ comfortable

Ⓑ huge

Ⓒ primitive

Ⓓ white

2. "Sometimes Ma would try to **console** her children."

CLUE: "She'd say, 'We got it good alongside those cotton slaves down South.'"

Ⓐ comfort

Ⓑ frighten

Ⓒ warm up

Ⓓ hide

3. "[Harriet] suffered from sleeping **spells**."

CLUE: "For the rest of her life, she had a deep dent in her head. . . . She could fall asleep while hoeing in the field or carrying a bucket of water from the well."

Ⓐ curses

Ⓑ nights

Ⓒ attacks

Ⓓ lessons

4. "John was quite **content** with his life."

CLUE: "It didn't bother John that he was not allowed to own land, vote, carry a gun, attend a church that had a black minister, or even own a dog. He just liked being called 'free.'"

Ⓐ unhappy

Ⓑ angry

Ⓒ excited

Ⓓ satisfied

Lincoln and the Sleeping Sentinel

by Peg Hall

It was a dark September morning in 1861. When I reached my office, some soldiers were waiting there for me. They were all talking at once, so I could understand nothing they said. One of them wore the bars of a captain.

[2] I said to them, "Boys, I cannot understand you. Please let your captain speak for you. Then I will do what I can."

[3] Their captain told me that they all belonged to Company K of the Third Vermont Regiment. They were from the slopes of the Green Mountains. Most of them were farm boys, and most of them were very young.

[4] After joining the army, they had been sent to Washington. Since arriving in July, they had been stationed at the Chain Bridge. It was about three miles away.

[5] The captain then told me the reason for their visit. The following is the story, as I understood it.

[6] William Scott was a mountain boy of Company K. He was a good fellow. So when another soldier was sick, William offered to fill in for him. He would take the other boy's picket duty. That meant he kept watch all night as the camp sentinel.

[7] The very next day, William found it was his turn to have picket duty. So he stood guard another night. But the boy couldn't stay awake two nights in a row. When his replacement came the next morning, William was asleep at his post.

[8] Falling asleep at your post was a crime in the army. The punishment for the crime was death. So William had a quick trial. He was found guilty and was to be shot.

[9] The boy's friends set out to save him. They called a meeting and

President Lincoln made time in 1862 to visit his soldiers in their camps.

came to me for advice. This was because I was also from Vermont. They had left camp in the morning and marched right to my office.

[10]I thought about the matter. It seemed hopeless, but I had to do something. And I had to do it right away—before I thought about it too much.

[11]"There is only one man who can help your friend," I said. "We will go see President Lincoln."

[12]I hurried off to the White House. William Scott's friends followed me. I didn't even stop to think about whether I was wrong to go to the president.

[13]When we got to the White House, the captain told his story again. He ended by saying, "William Scott is as brave as any boy in your army, Mr. President. There is no reason to shoot him like a dog."

[14]Lincoln's face was sad. In fact, I thought I saw a tear in his eye. But then he smiled. He asked me, "Do

A Very UnCivil War

your Green Mountain boys fight as well as they talk? If so, I believe all the stories I've heard about them."

[15]Then President Lincoln said, "But what can I do? You know I don't really give orders to the army."

[16]"I don't know, sir," I said. "I just knew it was no use going to General Smith. The only hope was to come to you. Maybe you could sign an order that Scott's case must be looked into and that he can't be shot before that happens. I could carry your order to the War Department."

[17]"No," said the president. "I don't think that would be safe. Army officers are a law unto themselves. They really think it's a good idea to shoot a soldier every once in a while.

[18]"I can understand why," Lincoln continued. "But only if the man runs away or commits a crime. Not for falling asleep when he's tired. The country has a better use for men than that.

[19]"Captain," said President Lincoln, "young Scott will not be shot. I will go to Chain Bridge myself to make sure."

[20]A few days later I saw a story in the newspaper. It said that a soldier had been pardoned by the president. And some time later I heard the whole story from William Scott. This is what he told me.

[21]"The president was the kindest man I had ever seen. At first I was afraid, for I had never met such a great man before. But he was so kind and gentle with me, I soon forgot my fright.

[22]"He asked about my home, the neighbors, the farm, and my friends. Then he asked about my mother. He told me I should never make her cry.

[23]"He didn't say a thing about the next day, when I was to be shot. I thought he was too kind to talk about it. But I wasn't sure why he told me not to make my mother cry. How could he say that when I was supposed to die the next morning? But I thought that was a question that would never get answered.

[24]"I just wanted to ask the president for one favor. I didn't want the firing party to be from my regiment. That would be the hardest thing of all—to die at the hands of my friends.

[25]"Just as I was going to ask him this favor, Mr. Lincoln stood up. He said, 'My boy, look me in the face.'

[26]"I did as he told me.

[27]" 'My boy,' he said, 'you are not going to be shot tomorrow. I believe you when you say you couldn't stay

awake. I am going to trust you and send you back to your regiment. Now I have a lot to do, and I had to take the time to come up here to see you. So I want to know what you are going to do to pay me back.'

[28]"I could hardly speak. I had expected to die, you see, so the idea of not dying took some getting used to. And it all changed in a minute!

[29]"But I managed to say, 'I am thankful, Mr. Lincoln—as thankful as any man can be. And I will find some way to pay you back. I can probably borrow some money from my parents. And payday is coming. My friends will help too. All together, I can give you five or six hundred dollars.'

[30]" 'But you owe me more than that,' he said.

[31]"I told him I didn't know how I would repay him, but I would find a way to do it.

[32]"Then Mr. Lincoln looked into my eyes. He said, 'My boy, the bill is a very large one. Your friends cannot pay it. Nor your parents. There is only one man who can pay it, and his name is William Scott. I will tell you how. From this day on, you must do your duty as a soldier. If you do that, the bill will be paid. Will you make that promise and keep it?'

[33]"I said I would. I could say no more. I wanted to tell him how hard I would try to do what he asked. But the words would not come.

[34]"He went away. And I never saw him again."

[35]The next part of this story takes place in March 1862. General Smith and his men were told to march to a spot near Yorktown.

[36]The general did as ordered. His force included Company K of the Third Vermont Regiment.

[37]The general's orders were to keep the Confederates from crossing the Warwick River. After a lively battle, the Confederates were pushed back.

[38]The mission should have ended there, but General McClellan arrived. He ordered Smith to take his men across the river. There they were to capture the Southern soldiers.

[39]The charge began late in the afternoon. The Vermonters held their guns over their heads. Then they dashed into and across the shallow river.

[40]There were far too many Confederates, and the Vermonters were quickly forced back. Almost half of them were left dead or hurt on the other shore.

[41]Every member of General Smith's forces was a brave man. But

A Very UnCivil War

all who were there agree about who was the bravest. It was William Scott of Company K. He was one of the first to reach the other side of the river. He was one of the last to turn back. And when he went back, he carried a hurt soldier with him.

[42]Then he returned to help others. No one is sure how many men he saved. But everyone agrees about what happened on his last trip across the river. The Confederates opened fire on him. William Scott was hit and fell to the shore.

[43]The rest of the story was told to me by one of Scott's friends. The following is what he said.

[44]"William was all shot to pieces. We carried him out of the line of fire. Then we laid him on the grass to die. He was bleeding all over. But he was a strong man and hard to kill.

[45]"The doctors patched him up.

[46]"We dropped on the ground to sleep. At daylight Scott asked to see us all. We went into the tent and stood around his bed. His face was bright, and his voice was cheerful.

[47]" 'Boys,' he said, 'I will never see another battle. This was my last. I haven't much to say. But you know what to tell them at home about me. I have tried to do the right thing. I am sure you will all say that.'

[48]"His voice was weak. He was dying. But then his face lit up. He spoke as clear as could be. 'I wish one of you could have the chance to tell President Lincoln something,' he said. 'Tell him that I never forgot his kind words. Tell him I have tried to be a good soldier—that I would have paid him back if I had lived. Tell him that I think of his kind face and thank him again. He gave me the chance to fall like a soldier in battle and not to die like a coward at the hands of my friends.' "

If you have been timing your reading speed for this story, record your time below.

_____ : _____

Minutes   Seconds

UNDERSTANDING THE MAIN IDEA

The following questions will demonstrate your understanding of what the story is about, or the *main idea*. Choose the best answer for each question.

1. This story is mainly about

- Ⓐ the harsh life of Union soldiers.
- Ⓑ how President Lincoln helped a young Union soldier.
- Ⓒ how Union soldiers saved their money to pay bills.
- Ⓓ the farmers in Vermont during the Civil War.

2. This story could have been titled

- Ⓐ "Paying a Debt to the President."
- Ⓑ "The Battle of Yorktown."
- Ⓒ "River Crossings During the Civil War."
- Ⓓ "A Confederate Is Spared."

3. Which detail best supports the main idea of this story?

- Ⓐ Picket duty was watching the camp all night.
- Ⓑ The Confederates opened fire on William Scott.
- Ⓒ General Smith and his men were told to march to a spot near Yorktown.
- Ⓓ As he was dying, William Scott thanked President Lincoln.

4. Find another detail that supports the main idea of this story. Write it on the lines below.

_____

_____

_____

RECALLING FACTS

The following questions will test how well you remember the facts in the story you just read. Choose the best answer for each question.

1. The punishment for falling asleep at one's post was

- Ⓐ life in prison.
- Ⓑ leading the next battle.
- Ⓒ death.
- Ⓓ being sent out of the army.

2. The narrator thought the only man who could help William Scott was

- Ⓐ President Lincoln.
- Ⓑ the narrator.
- Ⓒ Scott's captain.
- Ⓓ General Smith.

3. President Lincoln told William Scott that he should

- Ⓐ run away and hide from General Smith.
- Ⓑ never make his mother cry.
- Ⓒ tell his story to the War Department.
- Ⓓ face up to his punishment like a man.

4. After the battle near Yorktown, William Scott

- Ⓐ fell asleep at his post again.
- Ⓑ was sent home to recover from his injuries.
- Ⓒ visited President Lincoln at the White House.
- Ⓓ died from his injuries.

A Very UnCivil War

READING BETWEEN THE LINES

An *inference* is a conclusion drawn from facts. A *generalization* is a general statement, idea, or rule that is supported by facts. Analyze the story by choosing the best answer to each question below.

1. **What conclusion can you draw from paragraph 8?**

   Ⓐ Soldiers could be punished very severely for their actions.

   Ⓑ The army didn't really care if soldiers fell asleep at night.

   Ⓒ Soldiers were not allowed to have picket duty two nights in a row.

   Ⓓ William Scott was very sorry for falling asleep.

2. **What conclusion can you draw from paragraph 14?**

   Ⓐ The president was never emotional.

   Ⓑ The president couldn't understand what the men from Company K were trying to tell him.

   Ⓒ The president had heard the Green Mountain boys were good fighters.

   Ⓓ The Green Mountain boys were famous for running away during battle.

3. **Write a generalization about President Lincoln that can be made after reading this story.**

   _____

   _____

   _____

   _____

   _____

   _____

   _____

   _____

   _____

   _____

   _____

4. **It can be inferred from the story that**

   Ⓐ the narrator had never met President Lincoln before.

   Ⓑ the narrator believed Scott paid his debt to President Lincoln.

   Ⓒ President Lincoln often spoke to Scott's mother.

   Ⓓ the Union army won the Civil War.

DETERMINING CAUSE AND EFFECT

Choose the best answers for the following questions to show the relationship between what happened in the story (*effects*) and why those things happened (*causes*).

1. **Because William Scott had two nights of picket duty in a row,**

   Ⓐ the narrator told President Lincoln that Scott should be shot.

   Ⓑ another soldier was ill.

   Ⓒ the Confederates were able to capture Scott's camp.

   Ⓓ he fell asleep during the second night of his watch.

2. **What happened because the narrator and William Scott's captain spoke to President Lincoln?**

   Ⓐ President Lincoln saved Scott's life.

   Ⓑ They were asked to come back to the White House for dinner.

   Ⓒ The president issued an order that soldiers couldn't be shot for falling asleep.

   Ⓓ The Green Mountain boys became very famous.

3. **Why did William Scott ask the president to make sure the firing party was from a different regiment?**

   Ⓐ The men in his regiment were not very good shots.

   Ⓑ He didn't want to die at the hands of his friends.

   Ⓒ He thought looking for another regiment would keep the president busy.

   Ⓓ He knew there weren't any other Union regiments nearby.

4. **Why did the president tell William Scott that he must do his duty as a soldier?**

   Ⓐ Lincoln thought that was the best way Scott could pay him back.

   Ⓑ He was angry that he had to come all the way from Washington to talk to Scott.

   Ⓒ Scott told the president that he wanted to go home to Vermont.

   Ⓓ Scott didn't have enough money to pay the president.

USING CONTEXT CLUES

Skilled readers can often find the meaning of unfamiliar words by using *context clues*. This means they study the way the words are used in the text.

Use the context clues in the excerpts below to determine the meaning of each **bold-faced** word. Then choose the answer that best matches the meaning of the word.

1. "[William Scott] would take the other boy's **picket** duty."

CLUE: ". . . he kept watch all night as the camp sentinel."

  Ⓐ strike
  Ⓑ fence
  Ⓒ guard
  Ⓓ building

2. "[A newspaper article] said that a soldier had been **pardoned** by the president."

CLUE: " 'My boy,' [the president] said, 'you are not going to be shot tomorrow.' "

  Ⓐ hurt
  Ⓑ escorted
  Ⓒ driven
  Ⓓ forgiven

3. "[The president said], 'My boy, the **bill** is a very large one.' "

CLUE: " 'Your friends cannot pay it. Nor your parents. There is only one man who can pay it . . .' "

  Ⓐ debt
  Ⓑ receipt
  Ⓒ act
  Ⓓ money

4. "The **charge** began late in the afternoon."

CLUE: "[The general] ordered Smith to take his men across the river. There they were to capture the Southern soldiers."

  Ⓐ order
  Ⓑ explosion
  Ⓒ attack
  Ⓓ accusation

Sojourner Truth

Freedom Leader

by Shirley Jordan

Sojourner looked up at the kind face of the tall, lanky man. From her side came the voice of her friend Lucy Colman.

[2]"President Lincoln, may I present Mrs. Sojourner Truth."

[3]President Lincoln bowed and shook Sojourner's hand.

[4]"I'm pleased to meet you," he said. "I've heard about your many speeches."

[5]The president's hand is hard and rough like mine, Sojourner thought. Here is a man who knows hard work.

[6]"You are a great man to my people," she said. "I cried with happiness when you signed the Emancipation Proclamation."

[7]She could hardly believe she was in the White House. Sojourner thought back. It had been a long road. She had started out with nothing. She had started out as a slave.

[8]As a child, she was called Belle Hardenburgh. But even that name was not really hers. Slave children had no last names of their own. They took the name of the family that owned them.

[9]In Belle's case, a Dutch family, the Hardenburghs, owned her. They moved to New York in the 1790s.

[10]Belle had 11 brothers and sisters, but she had known only one brother, Peter. All her older brothers and sisters had been sold when they were very young.

[11]When she was 12, she had to stand on the small platform called an auction block. Her mother had no way to save her. But her mother said, "When you are afraid, talk to God."

[12]On the auction block, Belle knew little of what was happening around her. She spoke only Dutch. In just a few minutes, she belonged

to a man named Mr. Neely. Soon she found herself walking down the road behind his wagon.

[13]The Neelys beat her often. Her next owners were kind. But a need for money forced them to sell her. And her new owner, Mr. Dumont, was the meanest yet. Whip marks soon covered Belle's back and arms.

[14]When she was in her late teens, Mr. Dumont forced her to marry another slave. His name was Tom, and he was much older than Belle.

[15]Belle continued to work hard in the fields. In time, she had five children. There were four daughters and one son.

[16]The marriage was not a happy one, but Belle loved her children deeply.

[17]Then something began happening, and New York's slaves knew little about it. In 1817, the state had passed a new law. It said that on July 4, 1827, all adult slaves in the state were to be freed. Their children must work for their masters until the girls were 25 and the boys were 28. Then they would be free too.

[18]Like many former slaves, Tom had no skills to earn a living. So Belle began working for white families. She cleaned their houses.

[19]She had a chance to move to New York City. Tom stayed behind.

He later died in poverty.

[20]Years went by. Belle worked hard as a housekeeper. She often remembered her mother's words.

[21]One night in 1843 she prayed, "Tell me what you want me to do, oh Lord. I see so many poor people around me—even poorer than I am."

[22]A feeling came over her. She felt that it was her duty to help other black people. She packed her clothes in a pillowcase. Then she began to walk. She didn't know where she would go, but she knew she would be safe.

[23]In New York and Massachusetts, white people set up outdoor churches. Belle began speaking to these groups. She walked from meeting to meeting.

[24]That's what I am, she thought. I'm a sojourner, a person who walks from place to place. That will be my new name. I will spread the truth about slavery.

[25]Then she picked "Truth" as the rest of her name.

[26]Sojourner found other people who were against slavery. They were called abolitionists. They demanded an end to slavery.

[27]Many Americans hated abolitionists. Plantation owners in the South wanted them silenced.

[28]Olive Gilbert asked to write Truth's story. The abolitionists sold the book at their meetings.

[29]A few years later, Truth met Harriet Beecher Stowe, the author of *Uncle Tom's Cabin*. Many Northerners who'd read it had turned against slavery.

[30]Mrs. Stowe so admired Sojourner Truth's work that she wrote an article about her. It appeared in *The Atlantic Monthly,* an important magazine.

[31]The article made Sojourner Truth famous in the United States and even in parts of Europe.

[32]At age 67, Truth met President Lincoln. His Emancipation Proclamation had freed Southern slaves in 1863.

[33]But freedom had a price. Within a year, 13,000 homeless blacks had walked to Washington, D.C., from the South. They had no jobs and no money. Few of them could read or write.

[34]Sojourner Truth wanted to help. A camp was set up on the banks of the Potomac River. It was called Freedmen's Village. Life was a bit better there. There was shelter—and there was hope.

[35]"Your children must go to school and learn to read," Truth told the families. "You women who worked in the fields must now learn to cook and clean. You should know how to take care of the sick. Your families need you."

[36]She trusted President Lincoln to help. The war was ending, so he would have more time to make a plan.

[37]Then everything went wrong. Six days after the end of the Civil War, the president was shot and killed.

[38]Truth had never been so sad. Even as a slave, the future had not looked this dark.

Many consider Uncle Tom's Cabin *one of the most influential books written in America.*

A Very UnCivil War

[39]Vice President Andrew Johnson became president. Truth traveled to the White House. President Johnson was polite, and he listened carefully. But he made no promises.

[40]Things were not improving for the former slaves in Washington, D.C. Most were willing to work, but they had no land. Farming was all they knew.

[41]Then Truth had an idea. The U.S. still owned great areas of land in the West. Why couldn't some of that be given to the former slaves? With the right tools, they could get a new start.

[42]She wrote letters to Congress. So did her friends. She asked people to sign petitions. The petitions asked Congress to help.

[43]Hundreds signed. All the petitions were sent to Washington, D.C.

[44]For four years, she traveled and spoke to the people. But Congress never took action to give up the land. At last, she became tired and ill.

[45]In 1883, she was too sick to continue her work. She died at 86. Her daughters were at her side.

[46]Sojourner Truth had not finished all she wanted to do, but she had tried her best. This poor slave girl had traveled the country. She had spoken the truth. She had met two presidents.

[47]And she had left her mark on history.

If you have been timing your reading speed for this story, record your time below.

_____ : _____

Minutes   **Seconds**

UNDERSTANDING THE MAIN IDEA

The following questions will demonstrate your understanding of what the story is about, or the *main idea*. Choose the best answer for each question.

1. This story is mainly about

- Ⓐ homeless people after the Civil War.
- Ⓑ Presidents Lincoln and Johnson.
- Ⓒ how one former slave tried to help others.
- Ⓓ the freeing of slaves in New York.

2. This story could have been titled

- Ⓐ "Slaves of the Dutch in New York."
- Ⓑ "One Woman's Fight to Help Her People."
- Ⓒ "The Friends of Sojourner Truth."
- Ⓓ "Johnson's Solution for the Homeless."

3. Which detail best supports the main idea of this story?

- Ⓐ Sojourner noticed that the president's hand was hard and rough like hers.
- Ⓑ When Sojourner was in her late teens, Mr. Dumont forced her to marry another slave.
- Ⓒ Sojourner felt that it was her duty to help other black people.
- Ⓓ Plantation owners in the South wanted abolitionists silenced.

4. Find another detail that supports the main idea of this story. Write it on the lines below.

_____

_____

_____

RECALLING FACTS

The following questions will test how well you remember the facts in the story you just read. Choose the best answer for each question.

1. Slave children were called

- Ⓐ by the names of the people who owned them.
- Ⓑ thiefs, beggars, and hoodlums by white children.
- Ⓒ by names of their own choosing.
- Ⓓ the "poor little babies" by their Dutch masters.

2. Sojourner was freed from slavery

- Ⓐ because she was needed to help soldiers in the Civil War.
- Ⓑ by her last master, Mr. Dumont.
- Ⓒ because she had too many children.
- Ⓓ by a law that freed slaves in New York.

3. Sojourner Truth chose her new name because

- Ⓐ her mother's name was Sojourner and her husband's last name was Truth.
- Ⓑ she walked from place to place, telling the truth about slavery.
- Ⓒ she read it in a magazine article and really liked it.
- Ⓓ that's what the abolitionists started calling her.

4. On another sheet of paper, draw a picture of the camp Sojourner started for freed slaves in Washington, D.C. Then explain, using complete sentences, why there were so many homeless former slaves.

A Very UnCivil War

READING BETWEEN THE LINES

An *inference* is a conclusion drawn from facts. A *generalization* is a general statement, idea, or rule that is supported by facts. Analyze the story by choosing the best answer to each question below.

1. What conclusion can you draw from paragraph 13?

Ⓐ All slave owners beat their slaves.

Ⓑ Some slaves worked for many different families.

Ⓒ Slaves were not worth much money.

Ⓓ It was illegal to use whips on a slave.

2. What conclusion can you draw from paragraph 33?

Ⓐ Former slaves thought there would be jobs in Washington, D.C.

Ⓑ Many former slave owners paid the slaves for their work.

Ⓒ Most slaves did not have anywhere to go after they were freed.

Ⓓ The president invited former slaves to Washington, D.C., to meet Sojourner.

3. What generalization can you make from this story?

Ⓐ Freed slaves did not care about others who were still slaves.

Ⓑ All slaves were taught many different skills.

Ⓒ When the slaves were freed, there were many jobs at factories in the North.

Ⓓ Many slave children were sold when they were very young.

4. It can be inferred from the story that

Ⓐ many people thought it was a good idea to give freed slaves land in the West.

Ⓑ white people were angry at Sojourner because white people wanted land in the West for themselves.

Ⓒ there wasn't enough land in the West for white and black settlers.

Ⓓ President Johnson didn't care what happened to former slaves.

DETERMINING CAUSE AND EFFECT

Choose the best answers for the following questions to show the relationship between what happened in the story (*effects*) and why those things happened (*causes*).

1. Because Sojourner had been owned by a Dutch family until she was 12, she

Ⓐ didn't have to work very hard.

Ⓑ traveled across the Atlantic Ocean several times.

Ⓒ could only speak Dutch.

Ⓓ was a very good housekeeper.

2. What happened because Sojourner's husband couldn't make a living?

Ⓐ She kicked him out of the house.

Ⓑ She started cleaning houses for money.

Ⓒ He went to trade school.

Ⓓ She moved to New York City.

3. Why did Sojourner pack up her clothes and start walking?

Ⓐ She felt she needed to help other black people.

Ⓑ President Lincoln asked her to come help him with the homeless in Washington, D.C.

Ⓒ She couldn't afford to pay her rent.

Ⓓ She didn't have a horse to ride.

4. Why did Sojourner become famous in the United States and in parts of Europe?

Ⓐ Former slaves told everyone they met about Sojourner Truth.

Ⓑ She established the first trade school for black Americans.

Ⓒ Harriet Beecher Stowe wrote an article about her work in an important magazine.

Ⓓ Her name appeared in one of the most popular books of the time, *Uncle Tom's Cabin*.

USING CONTEXT CLUES

Skilled readers can often find the meaning of unfamiliar words by using *context clues*. This means they study the way the words are used in the text.

Use the context clues in the excerpts below to determine the meaning of each **bold-faced** word. Then choose the answer that best matches the meaning of the word.

1. "[Tom] later died in **poverty**."

CLUE: "Like many former slaves, Tom had no skills to earn a living."

  Ⓐ freedom

  Ⓑ happiness

  Ⓒ old age

  Ⓓ absence of money

2. "Mrs. Stowe so admired Sojourner Truth's work that she wrote an **article** about her."

CLUE: "It appeared in *The Atlantic Monthly,* an important magazine."

  Ⓐ story

  Ⓑ piece of clothing

  Ⓒ part of a Congressional bill

  Ⓓ little bit

3. "Even as slave, [Sojourner thought,] the future had not looked this **dark**."

CLUE: "Then everything went wrong. . . . Truth had never been so sad."

  Ⓐ black

  Ⓑ shaded

  Ⓒ bleak

  Ⓓ dim

4. "[Sojourner] asked people to sign **petitions**."

CLUE: "She wrote letters to Congress. So did her friends. . . . The petitions asked Congress to help."

  Ⓐ autographs

  Ⓑ books

  Ⓒ names

  Ⓓ pleas

Clara Barton

Angel of the Battlefield

by Julie Cahalan

Civil War soldiers faced many dangers. Disease was everywhere. There was little food. Many men did not have warm clothing or shoes. If a soldier was injured in battle, he probably would not receive proper treatment. Bandages were likely to be dirty. Little water or soap for washing was available. Medicine was scarce.

[2]As soldiers lay injured on the battlefield, a compassionate nurse moved among them. She brought clean bandages, fresh water, and hot food. She cleaned their wounds, filled their stomachs, and listened to their fears. Who was this lady of mercy who brought comfort to the injured and dying?

[3]Clara Barton, who became known as the "Angel of the Battlefield," was born on Christmas Day in 1821. She was the youngest of five children.

[4]Clara's parents believed in freedom for slaves, equal rights for women, quality education, and charity. Both of her parents were outspoken, and they often disagreed. Although Clara inherited her parents' values, she was quiet. She liked to play and work alone.

[5]Clara did well in school. She enjoyed boyish games with her brothers. Above all, she liked taking care of others.

[6]When she was 11, one of her brothers fell from the rafters of a barn. For two years, Clara took care of him. She also began helping children with their lessons. Clara even nursed poor families during a smallpox outbreak.

[7]When Clara grew up, she taught school. Many times, she didn't get paid. Her students' families had no money. But Clara felt the children deserved an education anyway.

Often, she urged towns to provide better schools and materials for their children. For a while, Clara went to college at one of the few schools that allowed women.

[8]In 1854, Clara and a friend went to Washington, D.C., to look for jobs. There weren't many for young women. Most women stayed home, married, and had babies. But Clara soon found a job. She did clerical work in the Patent Office. Clara copied papers, which was done by hand in the 1850s.

[9]Clara was working for the Patent Office when the Civil War began in 1861. In her spare time, she collected supplies for the soldiers. When injured soldiers were sent to Washington, D.C., Clara helped nurse them.

[10]Clara realized she was needed more on the battlefields than in the Patent Office. She began to help injured soldiers. The U.S. government then paid her to nurse the wounded rather than copy papers.

[11]Many officers thought Clara should not be there. They felt women belonged at home or with other women. Clara talked to the officers and persuaded them. She would deliver supplies and assist at a field hospital.

[12]On August 2, 1861, Clara delivered supplies to Fredericksburg. She was angry about the dirty hospital and the delay of needed supplies. She saw the same conditions at the next field hospital. Although she was appalled by what she saw, Clara went to work. She made food and bandages. She held hands and comforted the wounded. She cleaned the patients and the hospital. She even helped the doctors.

[13]Throughout the long days and years of the Civil War, Clara went from battlefield to battlefield. She helped the injured in hospitals and those lying on the ground.

[14]In August of 1862, a large battle was fought at Bull Run. When Clara arrived, she discovered that many of the injured had received no food or water for two days. They had been lying in the blazing sun. Clara made cornmeal mush with what supplies she had. After that was gone, she fed the men a mixture of crushed biscuits, wine, water, and brown sugar. Clara knew that the men would die without some sort of nourishment. She used whatever she could find to feed them.

[15]For two days, Clara had no rest or food while she worked among the men. Clean clothes and bandages

Wounded soldiers crowded Civil War hospitals.

[18]Clara assisted the doctors at Antietam. She helped surgeons amputate limbs from screaming soldiers. She even removed a bullet from the face of a young soldier with her pocketknife. Offering water to another soldier, Clara held his face to help him drink. A bullet then went through her sleeve, hitting the already wounded young man.

[19]One of the surgeons' wives, Mrs. Dunn, noticed Clara's hard work. She thought Clara performed her tasks dutifully and tirelessly. Mrs. Dunn said Clara was "the true heroine of the age, the angel of the battlefield."

[20]Later in 1862, Clara got typhoid fever. She took a month off and recuperated in Washington, D.C. As soon as she was able, Clara rejoined the army. She followed them from battle to battle and from camp to camp.

could save some lives. Kind words and encouragement might save others. For those beyond help, Clara just listened or gave last rites.

[16]In mid-September of that year, Clara was joined by two other women at the Harpers Ferry and South Mountain battlefields. Although they were a help to her, she didn't enjoy telling them what to do. She still had a quiet nature and preferred to do the work herself.

[17]Soon afterward, Clara helped at Antietam. A very bloody battle was taking place there. She was becoming used to seeing the horrendous wounds of the injured.

[21]Clara spent the rest of the war assisting soldiers of both sides. Countless wounded men, whether they were wearing blue or gray, took comfort from her nursing. In the midst of such death and destruction, her presence was often compared to that of an angel of mercy.

[22]When the war was over, Clara felt her work was far from done. She

was just beginning a lifelong pursuit of care for the injured, homeless, and outcast.

[23]One of her first projects after the Civil War was to help find missing soldiers. Many men had died in prison camps or in battle. Others couldn't be found. Their families were waiting for word of them.

[24]Clara realized that other soldiers often knew what had become of these men. She posted lists of missing soldiers in newspapers and post offices. The project was a success. Numerous soldiers were reunited with their families.

[25]With the aid of a former prisoner, Clara also identified the graves of nearly 13,000 men who had died in Andersonville. Andersonville was the largest Confederate prison camp. Men had been buried in unmarked trenches. In the end, all but 400 graves were identified and given proper headstones.

[26]Throughout her life, Clara Barton worked for suffering people. She spent several years in Europe, working with the Red Cross organization to help victims of war. Three countries awarded Clara medals for her efforts.

[27]Clara tried to start a similar charity in the United States. She wanted the American Red Cross to help victims of natural disasters, as well as those of war. She also wanted to help people be better prepared for either event.

[28]In 1881, the first chapter of the American Red Cross opened. It eventually became a nationwide relief agency. By the time she died, Clara had also introduced the idea of first aid training and helped develop the original first aid kits. Her work as an angel of mercy had gone far beyond the Civil War battlefields.

If you have been timing your reading speed for this story, record your time below.

_____ : _____

Minutes   *Seconds*

UNDERSTANDING THE MAIN IDEA

The following questions will demonstrate your understanding of what the story is about, or the *main idea*. Choose the best answer for each question.

1. This story is mainly about

Ⓐ diseases during the Civil War.

Ⓑ how to get inventions patented.

Ⓒ the work of a nurse on Civil War battlefields.

Ⓓ female soldiers in the Civil War.

2. This story could have been titled

Ⓐ "How the Red Cross Can Help You."

Ⓑ "Dying on the Field of Honor."

Ⓒ "U.S. Patent Processes."

Ⓓ "A Caring Nurse."

3. Which detail best supports the main idea of this story?

Ⓐ Civil War soldiers faced many dangers.

Ⓑ Clara Barton was working for the Patent Office when the Civil War began in 1861.

Ⓒ Clara Barton performed her duties as a nurse dutifully and tirelessly.

Ⓓ In 1881, the first chapter of the American Red Cross opened.

4. Find another detail that supports the main idea of this story. Write it on the lines below.

_____

_____

_____

RECALLING FACTS

The following questions will test how well you remember the facts in the story you just read. Choose the best answer for each question.

1. When injured soldiers were sent to Washington, D.C., Clara Barton

Ⓐ helped nurse them.

Ⓑ put them on trains to their hometowns.

Ⓒ read books to them.

Ⓓ asked them to work for the Patent Office.

2. Clara Barton persuaded army officers to

Ⓐ stop shooting when the sun set each evening.

Ⓑ allow her to nurse injured soldiers on the battlefields.

Ⓒ send their wounded men to her house.

Ⓓ serve healthier meals in their camps.

3. During the Civil War, Clara Barton

Ⓐ only helped Union soldiers.

Ⓑ spied on the Confederates for the Union army.

Ⓒ helped runaway slaves escape.

Ⓓ saved as many lives as she could, Union and Confederate.

4. Later in her life, Clara Barton started

Ⓐ to suffer attacks of malaria.

Ⓑ to write down what she had seen during the Civil War.

Ⓒ the American Red Cross.

Ⓓ buying land in the West for Civil War veterans.

A Very UnCivil War

READING BETWEEN THE LINES

An *inference* is a conclusion drawn from facts. A *generalization* is a general statement, idea, or rule that is supported by facts. Analyze the story by choosing the best answer to each question below.

1. **What conclusion can you draw from paragraphs 6–7?**

   (A) Clara enjoyed helping other people.

   (B) Clara disliked nursing her injured brother.

   (C) Smallpox was a common disease in Clara's town.

   (D) Most of Clara's students came from wealthy families.

2. **What conclusion can you draw from paragraph 12?**

   (A) Fredericksburg had the dirtiest field hospital in the country.

   (B) Clara thought cleaner hospitals would help soldiers get well.

   (C) There were a lot of women volunteering at field hospitals.

   (D) Clara was the only person at the hospital who could cook.

3. **What generalization can you make from this story?**

   (A) Most of the Civil War wounded liked having Clara nurse them.

   (B) Women were never allowed to leave their homes during Civil War battles.

   (C) All the doctors refused Clara's help on the battlefield.

   (D) No soldiers would tell their families about Clara when they got home.

4. **It can be inferred from the story that**

   (A) Union soldiers were more likely to be wounded than Confederate soldiers.

   (B) there was plenty of food for the soldiers from surrounding farms.

   (C) doctors weren't that busy at field hospitals.

   (D) doctors were not able to keep field hospitals clean.

DETERMINING CAUSE AND EFFECT

Choose the best answers for the following questions to show the relationship between what happened in the story (*effects*) and why those things happened (*causes*).

1. Because Clara Barton saw that wounded soldiers had not received food or water, she

   Ⓐ told the officers that they had to provide more food for their soldiers.

   Ⓑ used whatever she could find to feed the soldiers.

   Ⓒ decided it was no use and went home.

   Ⓓ asked farmers nearby to bring cornmeal and wheat to the field.

2. What happened because Clara Barton got typhoid fever?

   Ⓐ One of the doctors' wives started doing Clara's work.

   Ⓑ Doctors decided to try to find a new cure for the disease.

   Ⓒ Clara had to take a month off to get better.

   Ⓓ Clara infected several wounded soldiers with typhoid fever.

3. On the lines below, write the effect for the following cause in the story.

CAUSE: Clara Barton realized that soldiers often knew what had happened to missing men.

_____

_____

_____

_____

_____

_____

_____

_____

4. Why did Clara Barton try to start an American Red Cross?

   Ⓐ The European Red Cross wanted her to.

   Ⓑ She knew that a Red Cross charity would employ many Civil War veterans.

   Ⓒ An American Red Cross would help her find missing soldiers.

   Ⓓ She wanted to help victims of war and natural disasters.

A Very UnCivil War

USING CONTEXT CLUES

Skilled readers can often find the meaning of unfamiliar words by using *context clues*. This means they study the way the words are used in the text.

Use the context clues in the excerpts below to determine the meaning of each **bold-faced** word. Then choose the answer that best matches the meaning of the word.

1. "Although [Clara] was **appalled** by what she saw, Clara went to work."

CLUE: "[Clara] was angry at the delay of needed supplies and the dirty hospital."

  Ⓐ horrified

  Ⓑ excited

  Ⓒ punched

  Ⓓ thrilled

2. "Clara knew that the men would die without some sort of **nourishment**."

CLUE: "When Clara arrived, she discovered that many of the injured had received no food or water for two days. . . . she fed the men a mixture of crushed biscuits, wine, water, and brown sugar."

  Ⓐ prayers

  Ⓑ medicine

  Ⓒ food

  Ⓓ help

3. "[Clara] was becoming used to seeing the **horrendous** wounds of the injured."

CLUE: "A very bloody battle was taking place . . . She helped surgeons amputate limbs from screaming soldiers."

  Ⓐ minor

  Ⓑ awful

  Ⓒ delicate

  Ⓓ facial

4. "[Clara] took a month off and **recuperated** in Washington, D.C."

CLUE: ". . . Clara got typhoid fever. . . . As soon as she was able, Clara rejoined the army."

  Ⓐ vacationed

  Ⓑ danced

  Ⓒ recovered

  Ⓓ worked

End-of-Unit Activities

1. **Choose two Civil War heroes from this unit. Fill in the Venn diagram below to identify how they were alike and different. Find at least four likenesses and four differences. Stretch your thinking and avoid such answers as "They were both living during the Civil War."**

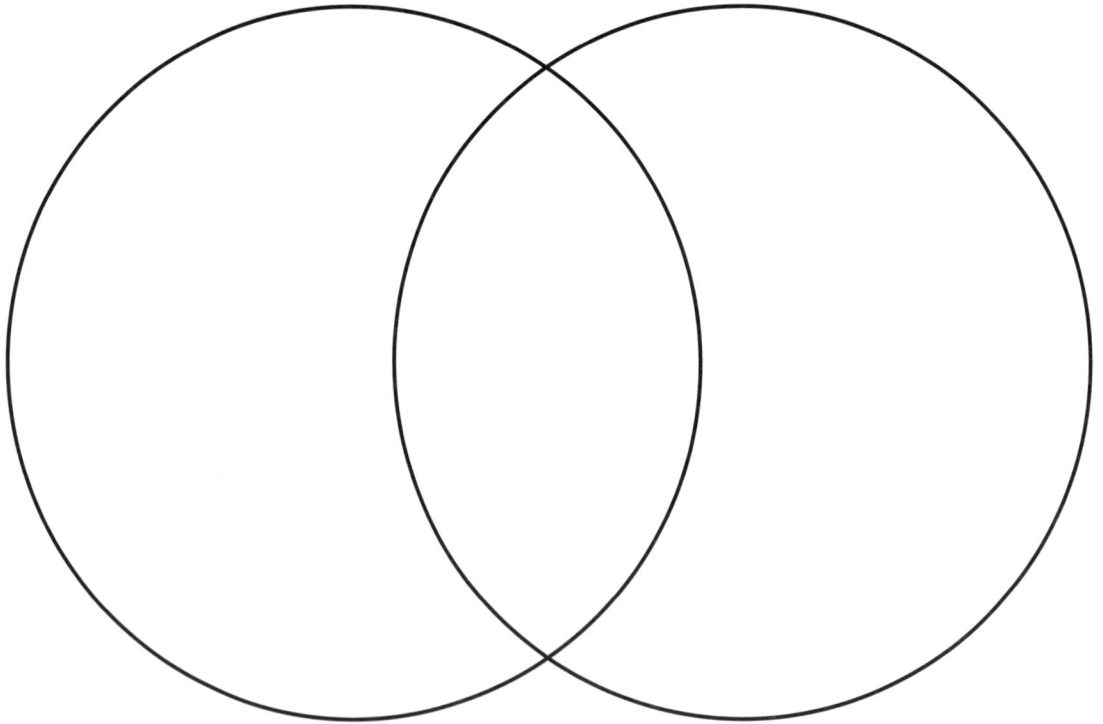

Hero #1   Hero #2

End-of-Unit Activities

2. Rank each of the stories in this unit, from the one you liked the most to the one you liked the least. For each story, write one interesting fact you learned. Then tell why you liked the story you ranked *1* the best.

LESSON 1 Ranking _____

_____

_____

_____

_____

LESSON 2 Ranking _____

_____

_____

_____

_____

LESSON 3 Ranking _____

_____

_____

_____

_____

LESSON 4 Ranking _____

_____

_____

_____

_____

Why did you like the story you ranked *1* the best?

_____

_____

_____

_____

Words-Per-Minute Chart

Directions:

Use the chart to find your words-per-minute reading speed. Refer to the reading time you recorded at the end of each article. Find your reading time in seconds along the left-hand side of the chart or minutes and seconds along the right-hand side of the chart. Your words-per-minute score will be listed next to the time in the column below the appropriate lesson number.

No. of Words	Lesson 1 1538	Lesson 2 1696	Lesson 3 1133	Lesson 4 1203	Minutes and Seconds
80	1154	1272	850	902	1:20
100	923	1018	680	722	1:40
120	769	848	567	602	2:00
140	659	727	486	516	2:20
160	577	636	425	451	2:40
180	513	565	378	401	3:00
200	461	509	340	361	3:20
220	419	463	309	328	3:40
240	385	424	283	301	4:00
260	355	391	261	278	4:20
280	330	363	243	258	4:40
300	308	339	227	241	5:00
320	288	318	212	226	5:20
340	271	299	200	212	5:40
360	256	283	189	201	6:00
380	243	268	179	190	6:20
400	231	254	170	180	6:40
420	220	242	162	172	7:00
440	210	231	155	164	7:20
460	201	221	148	157	7:40
480	192	212	142	150	8:00
500	185	204	136	144	8:20
520	177	196	131	139	8:40
540	171	188	126	134	9:00
560	165	182	121	129	9:20
580	159	175	117	124	9:40
600	154	170	113	120	10:00
620	149	164	110	116	10:20
640	144	159	106	113	10:40
660	140	154	103	109	11:00
680	136	150	100	106	11:20
700	132	145	97	103	11:40
720	128	141	94	100	12:00
740	125	138	92	98	12:20
760	121	134	89	95	12:40
780	118	130	87	93	13:00
800	115	127	85	90	13:20
820	113	124	83	88	13:40
840	110	121	81	86	14:00

(Seconds along left-hand side; Minutes and Seconds along right-hand side)

A Very UnCivil War

risking it all
for freedom

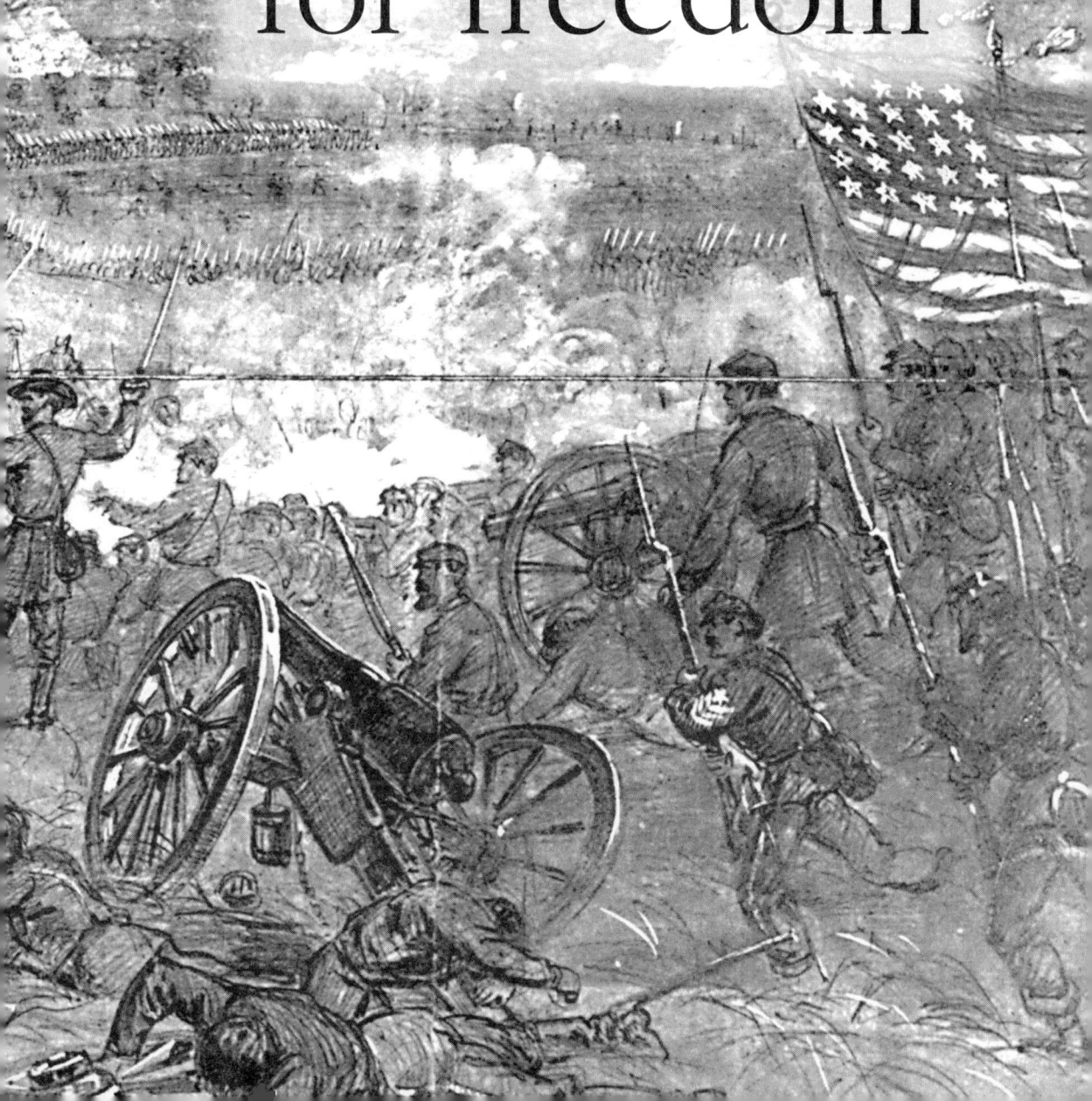

The Clothesline Telegraph

by Peg Hall

Major General Joe Hooker led Union troops.

[1]It was the early part of 1863. General Hooker and his Union troops were camped at Falmouth. The town was on the north bank of the Rappahannock River.

[2]The Union soldiers kept a close watch along the riverbank. For just across the river was the town of Fredericksburg. A large company of Confederate soldiers was camped there.

[3]All the scouts and guards of the Union army were very clever. They seemed to always know what was going on in the enemy camp. But here, as in other places, they had some help. This help came from two quick-thinking African American camp attendants.

[4]This story shows just how much those attendants did. It shows how clever they were at communicating through signals—signals that had meaning only to them.

[5]One day an African American man showed up at the Union camp. His name was Dabney, and he was looking for work. Dabney explained that he had come from a farm on the other side of the river. He said his wife had come along with him.

[6]Dabney knew an amazing amount about the countryside. He knew every mile of the river and the land along its banks, so the Union army was quick to hire him. General Hooker put him to work as a camp cook and servant.

[7]As he moved about camp, Dabney saw the army flag telegraph system. He was very interested in the system and how it worked. He begged the telegraph operators to explain the signs to him.

[8]So the operators did. They soon found that Dabney could understand

A Very UnCivil War

everything. In fact, he remembered what the signs meant as well as any of the operators did.

[9]Now there was a Southern woman in the camp who was going to be sent across the river to join the Southern troops. General Hooker was getting together a party to take her to Fredericksburg.

[10]Dabney's wife came to the general. She said that she wanted to be a servant for this lady. She would go with her across the river and live in the Confederate camp.

[11]The general didn't understand why Dabney's wife wished to leave, or why Dabney didn't ask her not to. But the general gave her permission to cross the river.

[12]So both women went across the Rappahannock to Fredericksburg. Within a few days Dabney's wife was a washerwoman. She worked at the headquarters of an important Confederate general. Robert E. Lee was his name.

[13]Dabney had stayed on the north side of the river in the Union camp. Before long it was clear that he knew a lot about what was going on across the river. No matter what the Confederates had planned, Dabney knew about it. If the Southern generals had a meeting, Dabney knew. If they talked about moving their troops, Dabney knew.

[14]Whatever Dabney knew, he told General Hooker. The general found out which rebel soldiers were moving or about to move. He found out where they were going and where they had been. He knew how long they had been marching. He even knew how many soldiers there were. And he knew it all because of Dabney. The servant's reports were always true.

[15]Yet Dabney never left the Union camp, and he never talked with the scouts who did leave. All of his time was spent doing his work as cook and servant.

[16]For quite a while, everyone was puzzled. How could Dabney know so much about what was going on in the Confederate camp? Many men asked him, but Dabney kept his secret—until at last he told his story to one of the Union officers.

[17]Dabney took the officer to the bank of the river. It was a spot with a clear view of Fredericksburg on the other side. Dabney pointed out a little cabin near the riverbank.

[18]"Do you see that clothesline there?" he asked. "The one with clothes drying on it?"

[19]"Yes, I see it," said the officer.

[20]"Well," said Dabney, "that's how I know. That clothesline tells me what goes on at Lee's headquarters."

[21]The officer looked at Dabney. He was clearly puzzled.

[22]"You see, my wife works over there," Dabney explained. "She washes and cooks for the officers. And she listens to everything they say.

[23]"As soon as she hears about anything going on, she comes to the clothesline. She moves the clothes around on the line. I can understand what she says in a minute."

[24]Well, the officer still didn't understand at all. How could Dabney tell anything from a clothesline?

[25]"My wife and I have our signals," continued Dabney. "We talked about them before she left. See that gray shirt?" Dabney pointed toward the clothesline. "That stands for General Longstreet. When she takes it off the line, it means he's gone to Richmond. The white shirt means General Hill. She's moved it to the north end of the line. So I know that Hill and his men have headed upstream. The red shirt is Stonewall Jackson. It's down on the right side now. If he moves, she will move that red shirt. That's how I know."

[26]The officer just shook his head. But Dabney kept checking his clothesline telegraph. He kept making his reports—and they were all true.

[27]One morning Dabney came to report movement in the rebel camp. "But it doesn't mean a thing," he said. "They aren't really going anywhere. They're just pretending."

[28]An officer went out to study the clothesline. There had been quite a shifting of shirts. Nothing on the line was where it had been earlier.

[29]The officer turned to Dabney. "How do you know there's nothing going on?" he asked.

[30]"Do you see those two blankets?" asked Dabney. "The

A Very UnCivil War

ones pinned together at the bottom?"

[31]"Yes," said the officer. "What of it?"

[32]"Why, that's my wife's way of making a fish trap," said Dabney. "She pinned the blankets together that way. She's telling me that General Lee is trying to draw us into a trap."

[33]So General Hooker paid no attention to the movements across the river.

[34]The two armies spent many weeks watching each other. The Union army sat on the north side of the river. The Confederate army sat on the south side of the river. And Dabney and his wife kept on using their clothesline telegraph. They were the quickest and best of all of General Hooker's scouts.

If you have been timing your reading speed for this story, record your time below.

_____ : _____

Minutes   **Seconds**

UNDERSTANDING THE MAIN IDEA

The following questions will demonstrate your understanding of what the story is about, or the *main idea*. Choose the best answer for each question.

1. This story is mainly about

Ⓐ how to dry clothes on a clothesline.

Ⓑ how an African American couple spied for the Union army.

Ⓒ how an African American couple spied for the Confederate army.

Ⓓ camp life along Rappahannock River.

2. This story could have been titled

Ⓐ "Spying on the Confederates."

Ⓑ "Shirts First, Pants Next, Blankets Last."

Ⓒ "The Army's Flag Telegraph System."

Ⓓ "The Camp Cook's Duties."

3. Which detail best supports the main idea of this story?

Ⓐ The town was on the north bank of the Rappahannock River.

Ⓑ Dabney knew an amazing amount about the countryside.

Ⓒ Dabney told an officer that the clothesline told him what was going on at Lee's headquarters.

Ⓓ The two armies spent many weeks watching each other.

4. Find another detail that supports the main idea of this story. Write it on the lines below.

_____

_____

_____

RECALLING FACTS

The following questions will test how well you remember the facts in the story you just read. Choose the best answer for each question.

1. Dabney and his wife asked for

Ⓐ work at the Union camp.

Ⓑ a safe place to sleep while the battles were close to their farm.

Ⓒ food for soldiers at the Confederate camp.

Ⓓ work for their sons under General Lee.

2. Dabney was very interested in

Ⓐ cooking for Confederate soldiers.

Ⓑ General Hooker's plans for battle.

Ⓒ the camp's flag telegraph system.

Ⓓ becoming an army officer.

3. Dabney's wife went to the Confederate camp with

Ⓐ letters from General Hooker.

Ⓑ a Southern woman.

Ⓒ General Hooker's wife.

Ⓓ some of General Lee's men.

4. Dabney's wife hung shirts on the clothesline

Ⓐ to get them dry.

Ⓑ whenever there was going to be a battle.

Ⓒ by knotting the sleeves together over the clothesline.

Ⓓ to show movement of Southern officers.

A Very UnCivil War

READING BETWEEN THE LINES

An *inference* is a conclusion drawn from facts. A *generalization* is a general statement, idea, or rule that is supported by facts. Analyze the story by choosing the best answer to each question below.

1. What conclusion can you draw from paragraph 5?

Ⓐ Dabney and his wife were free African Americans.

Ⓑ Dabney and his wife had been successful farmers before the war.

Ⓒ Dabney was really a Confederate spy.

Ⓓ The Union army hired a lot of African Americans.

2. What conclusion can you draw from paragraphs 22–23?

Ⓐ The Confederate officers talked in a secret code Dabney's wife could understand.

Ⓑ Dabney's wife did the Confederate officers' laundry once a week.

Ⓒ The Confederate officers made sure they had clean shirts before they left camp.

Ⓓ The Confederate officers didn't watch Dabney's wife very closely.

3. What generalization can you make from this story?

Ⓐ All army camps hired servants to perform chores.

Ⓑ There were no African American soldiers in the Union camp.

Ⓒ Enemy armies sometimes camped within sight of each other without fighting.

Ⓓ Confederates never allowed African Americans in their camps.

4. It can be inferred from the story that

Ⓐ the Union army paid its cooks very well.

Ⓑ the Union army needed people who knew the countryside.

Ⓒ the Union scouts weren't very good at finding out information.

Ⓓ the Rappahannock River was very wide.

———— ■ ————

DETERMINING CAUSE AND EFFECT

Choose the best answers for the following questions to show the relationship between what happened in the story (*effects*) and why those things happened (*causes*).

1. **Because Dabney knew a lot about the area around the Union camp,**

   Ⓐ General Hooker tied him up and asked him a lot of questions.

   Ⓑ General Hooker thought he was a spy.

   Ⓒ General Hooker was quick to hire him to work in camp.

   Ⓓ General Hooker wanted to hire Dabney's wife.

2. **What happened because a Southern lady wanted to join the Confederate camp?**

   Ⓐ General Hooker made her become a laundry worker.

   Ⓑ General Hooker had some men escort her across the river.

   Ⓒ General Hooker made a reservation for her on the ferry.

   Ⓓ General Hooker asked General Lee to come and get her.

3. **Why did General Hooker know so much about the Confederate camp?**

   Ⓐ General Hooker and General Lee were very good friends.

   Ⓑ Some of the Confederate soldiers used the flag telegraph system to send messages to General Hooker.

   Ⓒ General Hooker's scouts were very good at finding out information.

   Ⓓ Dabney told General Hooker whatever he found out from his wife.

4. **Why did Dabney's wife pin two blankets together on the clothesline?**

   Ⓐ She was trying to keep them from blowing away in the wind.

   Ⓑ She wanted Dabney to know the Confederate soldiers were cold.

   Ⓒ She was telling Dabney that General Lee wanted to trap the Union army.

   Ⓓ She only had enough clothespins to hold one blanket on the clothesline.

USING CONTEXT CLUES

Skilled readers can often find the meaning of unfamiliar words by using *context clues*. This means they study the way the words are used in the text.

Use the context clues in the excerpts below to determine the meaning of each **bold-faced** word. Then choose the answer that best matches the meaning of the word.

1. "This help came from quick-thinking African American camp **attendants**."

CLUE: "General Hooker put him to work as a camp cook and servant."

   Ⓐ counselors

   Ⓑ companies

   Ⓒ workers

   Ⓓ guards

2. "As he moved about camp, Dabney saw the army flag **telegraph** system."

CLUE: "He begged the telegraph operators to explain the signs to him."

   Ⓐ signal

   Ⓑ charting

   Ⓒ wire

   Ⓓ color

3. "General Hooker was getting together a **party** to take [a Southern woman] to Fredericksburg."

CLUE: "Now there was a Southern woman in the camp who was going to be sent across the river to join the Southern troops."

   Ⓐ celebration

   Ⓑ group

   Ⓒ individual

   Ⓓ side

4. "But the general gave [Dabney's wife] **permission** to cross the river." (paragraph 11)

Write what you think the bolded word means. Then record the context clues that led you to this definition.

Meaning:

_____

_____

_____

Context clues:

_____

_____

_____

Belle Boyd the Spy

by Peg Hall

¹During and after the War Between the States, tales were told of brave deeds. There were heroes on both sides of the fight. They were Northerners and Southerners, men and women.

²This is the tale of a brave woman of the South. Her name was Belle Boyd.

³The story begins when Belle was just a girl. The Union army had taken over the town where she lived. Belle's father was away fighting for the South. Belle and her mother had been left to keep their home safe.

⁴One morning Belle was upstairs. She heard her mother give a frightened cry. At once Belle grabbed a gun from under her bed. Her father had given it to her before he left. She hid it under her long skirt and flew downstairs.

⁵There, she found her mother fighting off a Union soldier.

⁶"Tell me where your Confederate flag is hidden!" the soldier cried.

⁷Belle's mother told him they had no flag, but the soldier wouldn't listen. There was talk in town, he said, talk that the Boyds were hiding a Confederate flag. And now that the Union army had taken over, that was against the law.

⁸Again Mrs. Boyd said there was no flag. But the angry soldier pushed her against the wall.

⁹"Let her go!" cried Belle.

¹⁰The soldier turned and smiled at her. He saw a young girl—nothing to fear. So he moved closer to Mrs. Boyd. He put one hand around the woman's thin arm.

¹¹"Didn't you hear me?" asked Belle in a low voice.

[12]"Be quiet!" snapped the soldier. "Pretty as you are, I'd sure hate to have to hurt you—and I might have to."

[13]He headed for the door. He was pulling Belle's mother along with him!

[14]That was all Belle needed to see. She took the gun out from under her dress.

[15]Belle called out one more warning, but the Union soldier kept moving.

[16]Belle lifted the gun in her shaking hands. Then she fired. The soldier dropped to the floor.

[17]"He's dead!" cried Mrs. Boyd. "Oh, Belle, what have you done? What will happen to us now?"

[18]"I don't know, Mother," said Belle. "I just know that we can't give up our flag. I have a strange feeling about it. I think that if we lose that flag, the South will lose the war."

[19]The next day Belle was brought before a captain in the Union army. "This is a serious charge, Miss Boyd," the captain said. "I could send you to prison. So tell me, why did you kill that soldier?"

[20]Belle kept her eyes on the floor. In a small voice, she told her story. She explained that the soldier had been hurting her mother.

[21]The Union captain studied the girl standing in front of him. She seemed small and helpless, not at all dangerous.

[22]The captain shook his head. He was a good man who hated war and loved his own mother. So he could understand what Belle had done.

[23]The captain reached into his desk drawer. He pulled out a small gun. "Here," he said. "You may need to protect your mother and yourself again. Next time, use this. But don't kill any more of my soldiers—not unless they are trying to hurt you. I'd not like to see this war won by a girl."

[24]Belle's lips smiled as she took the gun, but her eyes were angry.

[25]Two years later the town was still under Union control. Belle was used to seeing soldiers on the streets and in the shops. And they were used to seeing Belle.

[26]The soldiers never saw anything to worry about in Belle. She was just a pretty girl who lived in town.

[27]But Belle kept her eyes and ears open. She became a spy for the South.

[28]It happened for the first time when some Union officers met in a hotel. Belle was there too, in a room above. She lay with her ear against the floor, listening.

[29]Belle heard loud voices and laughter. Then a door slammed, and Belle's heart beat faster. What if they found her? she thought. She would be shot as a spy!

[30]Still, she kept on listening. For a time nothing important was said. But then she heard the voice of General Banks, a Union leader.

[31]"Here," he said. "Look on the map. This is where Stonewall Jackson and his army will be. I will lead my men to a spot in front of Jackson. The rest of you will come around from the back. We will have him trapped in a pocket."

[32]Belle held her breath and listened. At last she heard the general tell where and when the trap would be set. She knew what she had to do.

[33]Belle went to work. She wrote letters to General Banks and each of his men. The letters invited them to a party.

[34]Belle delivered the letters. Then she hurried from the hotel. She found a fast horse and headed for the mountains. She knew that was where General Stonewall Jackson was camped.

[35]It was a dark, windy night. At first Belle was frightened. There was no one else out. It was against the law to be outside after dark without a special pass. And passes were hard to get.

[36]Belle had a pass, but it wasn't really hers. If anyone checked it, he or she would know. And then that person would know that she was a spy.

[37]If that happened, Belle would be killed, for that was the fate of any spy.

[38]Still, Belle went on. She had to get to Stonewall Jackson and back before daylight.

[39]Suddenly, she heard a shout. "Halt! Who goes there?"

[40]It was a Union soldier!

[41]Belle pulled the horse to a stop. "I have a pass," she said in a shaking voice. "My aunt is sick. I'm just going to visit her."

[42]Slowly, she reached into her pocket, but the soldier didn't wait to see her pass. He just waved her on. After all, she was just a girl. She couldn't be dangerous.

[43]Before long Belle reached Jackson's camp. She gave her message, then left. The sun was just coming up when she got back to town.

[44]The night of the party arrived. Belle was there to greet her guests.

A Very UnCivil War

She wore a lovely dress—and a warm smile.

[45]The Union officers thought Belle smiled because of the party, but she had other reasons for being happy.

[46]Soon the music started. All the officers wanted to dance with Belle. And dance she did. She danced as if she hadn't a care in the world.

[47]General Banks himself had been watching her. At last he asked her to dance. As the music started up again, they swept out onto the floor.

[48]"This is a lovely party, Miss Boyd," the general said. "And you are equally lovely."

[49]Belle smiled and said a soft thank-you.

[50]"So I guess you can see that Union soldiers aren't all bad," the general said. Belle didn't answer.

[51]"You Confederate ladies surely know how to put on a party," the general went on. "You are far better at that than your men are at fighting."

[52]The general began to laugh. Belle stopped dancing. She was angry, but she was trying to hide her feelings.

[53]"You must excuse me, General," she said with a smile. "I have something I want to give you."

[54]Belle left the general in the middle of the dance floor. She hurried from the room.

[55]When Belle returned, she had a folded piece of cloth in her arms.

[56]"For you, General," said Belle with a laugh. Then she threw the cloth over his head. As it unfolded, everyone could see what it was—a Confederate flag!

[57]Suddenly the door flew open, and in ran Confederate soldiers! Their guns were drawn and ready to fire.

[58]The Union soldiers didn't have guns with them. After all, they were at a party. Some ran off to get their guns. Others ran to get away. All those who ran were killed on the spot.

[59]The room was filled with the sounds of shots and screams. Some of the ladies fainted. But others—all Southerners—smiled.

[60]At last the room was quiet. The Union men were lined up and marched out of the room.

[61]As General Banks passed, Belle smiled.

[62]"How is this for being caught in a pocket, General?" she asked.

[63]The general stared at Belle in surprise. He could hardly believe she was using the very words he had used. She had set the trap before he could!

[64]A few weeks later, Belle Boyd got a note from General Stonewall Jackson. In it, he thanked her for her bravery.

[65]For the rest of the war, Belle kept the note in a safe place—right next to her Confederate flag.

If you have been timing your reading speed for this story, record your time below.

_____ : _____

Minutes   **Seconds**

*A Very Un*Civil *War*

UNDERSTANDING THE MAIN IDEA

The following questions will demonstrate your understanding of what the story is about, or the *main idea*. Choose the best answer for each question.

1. This story is mainly about

Ⓐ General Banks's plans to trap General Jackson.

Ⓑ spies in the Union army.

Ⓒ a girl who spied for the Confederate army.

Ⓓ parties Union soldiers attended in the South.

2. This story could have been titled

Ⓐ "The Final Shot."

Ⓑ "The Unlikely Spy."

Ⓒ "Girls Who Spied in the Civil War."

Ⓓ "Party at Belle's House."

3. Which detail best supports the main idea of this story?

Ⓐ The Union army had taken over the town where Belle lived.

Ⓑ Belle Boyd's mother told a Union soldier that they had no Confederate flag.

Ⓒ Belle wore a lovely dress to the party.

Ⓓ Belle lay with her ear to the floor, listening.

4. Find another detail that supports the main idea of this story. Write it on the lines below.

_____

_____

_____

RECALLING FACTS

The following questions will test how well you remember the facts in the story you just read. Choose the best answer for each question.

1. Belle Boyd's father was away from home because

Ⓐ he was in Europe on business.

Ⓑ the Union soldiers had sent him to a prison camp.

Ⓒ he was fighting for the South.

Ⓓ he was chasing some escaped slaves.

2. The soldier wanted Belle Boyd's mother to give him

Ⓐ a Confederate flag he'd heard she had hidden.

Ⓑ a going-away party before he left town.

Ⓒ some horses for the Union army.

Ⓓ the secret password that General Jackson used.

3. The first time Belle Boyd spied on Union soldiers, she

Ⓐ got caught.

Ⓑ overheard soldiers in a hotel talking.

Ⓒ talked a Union captain into giving her a gun.

Ⓓ was having a party for them.

4. Belle Boyd surprised General Banks by

Ⓐ telling him where General Jackson was camped.

Ⓑ giving him money she'd raised for supplies.

Ⓒ shooting him with the gun a Union captain gave her.

Ⓓ throwing a Confederate flag over his head.

READING BETWEEN THE LINES

An *inference* is a conclusion drawn from facts. A *generalization* is a general statement, idea, or rule that is supported by facts. Analyze the story by choosing the best answer to each question below.

1. What conclusion can you draw from paragraphs 15–16?

   Ⓐ The shot scared the soldier and he fainted.

   Ⓑ Belle didn't want the soldier to know she was there.

   Ⓒ Belle killed the soldier.

   Ⓓ Belle signaled some other soldiers to help her.

2. What conclusion can you draw from paragraph 31?

   Ⓐ General Banks knew General Jackson's plans.

   Ⓑ Jackson and Banks had agreed to meet to discuss ending the war.

   Ⓒ Banks planned to throw a net over Jackson and capture him.

   Ⓓ Jackson was several days' march away from Banks and his men.

3. What generalization can you make from this story?

   Ⓐ There were no other women who spied for the South.

   Ⓑ Union soldiers didn't expect pretty, young girls to be spies.

   Ⓒ All Southern women knew how to shoot guns.

   Ⓓ Union soldiers often attended parties held by Southern families.

4. It can be inferred from the story that

   Ⓐ Belle had never met General Banks before the party.

   Ⓑ Belle knew General Banks really wanted a Confederate flag as a keepsake.

   Ⓒ General Banks and his men were too busy working to go to a party.

   Ⓓ Belle had met General Banks before she overheard him at the hotel.

A Very UnCivil War

DETERMINING CAUSE AND EFFECT

Choose the best answers for the following questions to show the relationship between what happened in the story (*effects*) and why those things happened (*causes*).

1. Because he'd heard that Belle Boyd and her mother had a Confederate flag, the soldier

Ⓐ made a law against keeping a Confederate flag.

Ⓑ tried to get Belle's mother to tell him where it was.

Ⓒ told Belle that she was a pretty girl.

Ⓓ went to a party at Belle's house.

2. What happened because Belle Boyd seemed small and helpless?

Ⓐ The Union soldier tried to keep her in a closet.

Ⓑ She was given a small pony to ride.

Ⓒ The Union soldiers let her shop wherever she wanted in town.

Ⓓ The Union captain gave her another gun to protect herself.

3. Why did Belle Boyd stop dancing with General Banks?

Ⓐ He kept stepping on her toes.

Ⓑ She was angry at what he said.

Ⓒ The music had stopped.

Ⓓ The general offered to get her a drink of lemonade.

4. Why did none of the Union soldiers suspect that Belle Boyd was a spy? Answer using complete sentences.

_____

_____

_____

_____

_____

_____

_____

_____

_____

_____

_____

_____

_____

_____

_____

_____

_____

_____

_____

USING CONTEXT CLUES

Skilled readers can often find the meaning of unfamiliar words by using *context clues*. This means they study the way the words are used in the text.

Use the context clues in the excerpts below to determine the meaning of each **bold-faced** word. Then choose the answer that best matches the meaning of the word.

1. " 'Be quiet!' **snapped** the soldier."

CLUE: "But the angry soldier pushed her against the wall. . . . 'Pretty as you are, I'd sure hate to have to hurt you—and I might have to.' "

   Ⓐ clipped

   Ⓑ shouted

   Ⓒ broke

   Ⓓ clicked

2. " 'This is a **serious** charge, Miss Boyd,' the captain said."

CLUE: " 'I could send you to prison.' "

   Ⓐ sober

   Ⓑ humorous

   Ⓒ critical

   Ⓓ thoughtful

3. "The letters invited [General Banks and his men] to a **party**."

CLUE: "Soon the music started. All the officers wanted to dance with Belle."

   Ⓐ celebration

   Ⓑ group

   Ⓒ individual

   Ⓓ side

4. "Suddenly, [Belle] heard a shout. **'Halt!'** "

CLUE: " 'Who goes there?' . . . Belle pulled the horse to a stop."

   Ⓐ "Hello!"

   Ⓑ "My goodness!"

   Ⓒ "It's hot!"

   Ⓓ "Stop!"

A Very UnCivil War

Charles Hopkins

American Hero

by Paula Reece

Union troops charged the Confederate lines at Gaines' Mill.

Charles Fern Hopkins knew compassion from the time he was very young. He grew up in a New Jersey home that was opposed to slavery. Their home was a station on the Underground Railroad.

[2]Many slaves stayed with the Hopkins family on their journeys to freedom. Charles also spent many dark nights driving slaves to their next "station." He didn't fear being caught, but he did fear disappointing his father.

[3]Charles heard about the firing upon Fort Sumter. He longed to serve his country. He left home without telling his father. At age 18, he joined the Union army as a private.

[4]Hopkins camped in Trenton, New Jersey, with the 1st New Jersey Volunteer Infantry. Some of his enthusiasm faded after he realized how boring and repetitive camp life could be. Hopkins soon learned how to have fun, though. He was young and mischievous. He quickly made friends with other young privates in the regiment.

[5]Finally, Hopkins' regiment left camp for Washington, D.C., and soon after was ordered to march to Vienna, Virginia. The men quickly realized that their provisions were not following them to their new camp. Hopkins and his friends disobeyed orders by searching the countryside for food.

[6]One time Hopkins and his friends were fired upon while picking blackberries. They ducked out of the way. Then they located the source of the gunfire. It was coming from an abandoned barn. Hopkins and his fellow comrades hadn't realized that enemy soldiers

had snuck inside. The Union soldiers quickly returned to camp.

[7] When Hopkins and his friends arrived at camp, members of their regiment showed great concern. They urged the men to lie down and asked if they were in great pain. Hopkins couldn't figure out why. None of them had been shot. Then Hopkins glanced down at his uniform and hands, and he understood.

[8] Their hands and faces were scratched from the thorns of the berry bushes. Their uniforms were torn. And the berry juice that stained their faces, hands, and uniforms resembled blood. No wonder the members of the 1st New Jersey were acting so strangely! It looked as if Hopkins and his friends had participated in a bloody battle. They shared a good laugh. For they had yet to fight in a real battle.

[9] They would get the chance to become true soldiers the following month. General Philip Kearny was appointed to take charge of their regiment.

[10] Kearny quickly earned the respect of his men. He was able to mold them into well-disciplined soldiers by the end of the summer. The general also made sure that his troops had proper uniforms and equipment. He paid for much of this out of his own pocket because supplies were slow to arrive.

[11] Kearny turned down one promotion. But eventually he could refuse no more. By late spring, he had to leave his well-trained and loyal men. However, he left behind the valuable skills he had taught them. These would help the regiment during the rest of the war.

[12] On June 27, the 1st New Jersey fought the Confederates in a heated battle at Gaines' Mill in Virginia. During the fight, Hopkins was hit twice by gunfire. As he retreated from the front line, he found one of his officers. The officer had a shattered leg. He asked for Hopkins' help in getting off the battlefield.

[13] Although wounded himself, Charles carried the officer on his back for more than 1,200 yards. He had to be careful not to be hit by the intense crossfire. To make it even more difficult, the officer was quite a bit taller than Hopkins. But Hopkins managed to get both to safety.

[14] Hopkins was temporarily blind and suffering from exhaustion. However, he refused to lie down and rest. He returned to the battlefield. Soon after, he was shot again. This time he was hit in the left side of the head. He fell to the

ground. His comrades thought he was dead. Miraculously, he came to and struggled to his feet. He waited patiently to have his wounds treated. He waited five days until the fighting slowed down.

[15]For the next year and a half, Charles was hospitalized. After his release, Charles convinced his doctor to let him return to his regiment. The Wilderness Campaign in Virginia began on May 4, 1864. A few days later, Hopkins was wounded. He was ordered to go to the field hospital, but he refused. He wanted to stay and help his regiment. Unfortunately, this decision had serious consequences. By the end of the day, Hopkins was captured.

[16]For two weeks, the prisoners were marched to an unknown destination. They were abused by their captors. Many soldiers who could not keep up the march were killed on the spot. Finally, on May 22, the prisoners arrived in Georgia at Andersonville, the military prison of the Confederacy.

Andersonville, the infamous Confederate prison, was located in southwest Georgia.

[17]Hopkins kept a journal. In it, he recorded what life was like in the prison. He survived thirst and dehydration, assaults by a gang known as the "Raiders," and the mental anguish of being away from his friends and family. Seeing men die became an everyday occurrence.

[18]Charles tried to escape twice by just walking out the gate. After the second attempt, he was tortured as an example to the other prisoners.

[19]In September, the prisoners were moved to other prisons. The Confederates feared that the Union army would attack Andersonville.

[20]By December, Hopkins was suffering from scurvy, but he had hope. A few prisoners were being released from prison. Hopkins' surgeon promised him he would soon be released. However, a married man begged to take Hopkins' turn. He was afraid he would never see his family again.

Hopkins' compassion did not allow him to turn the man down.

[21]At the end of February, the Confederates agreed to release the rest of the prisoners. Hopkins had been unconscious for 20 days due to typhoid fever. But he managed to crawl out of the building to freedom.

[22]After being reunited with his family, Hopkins had to work to regain his health. He then went on to return to his family's harness-making business, get married, and have children. He honored his fellow comrades at Andersonville by erecting the first state monument at Andersonville National Cemetery. At the age of 85, he was awarded the Congressional Medal of Honor for his heroism at Gaines' Mill, Virginia.

[23]Charles Hopkins was a true American hero, a man who put his country and his fellow humans ahead of himself.

If you have been timing your reading speed for this story, record your time below.

_____ : _____

Minutes   *Seconds*

A Very UnCivil War

UNDERSTANDING THE MAIN IDEA

The following questions will demonstrate your understanding of what the story is about, or the *main idea*. Choose the best answer for each question.

1. This story is mainly about

Ⓐ a heroic Confederate soldier.

Ⓑ a heroic Union soldier.

Ⓒ the lack of supplies during the Civil War.

Ⓓ the spread of disease during the Civil War.

2. This story could have been titled

Ⓐ "Boring Camp Life."

Ⓑ "Searching for Food."

Ⓒ "An Unselfish Soldier."

Ⓓ "Captured by the Union!"

3. Which detail best supports the main idea of this story?

Ⓐ Many slaves stayed with the Hopkins family on their journeys to freedom.

Ⓑ Hopkins camped in Trenton, New Jersey, with the 1st New Jersey Volunteer Infantry.

Ⓒ Gunfire came from an abandoned barn.

Ⓓ Although wounded himself, Charles carried an officer on his back for more than 1,200 yards.

4. Find another detail that supports the main idea of this story. Write it on the lines below.

_____

_____

_____

RECALLING FACTS

The following questions will test how well you remember the facts in the story you just read. Choose the best answer for each question.

1. At age 18, Charles Hopkins

Ⓐ joined the Union army.

Ⓑ joined the rebel forces.

Ⓒ opened his own business.

Ⓓ got married.

2. During his first battle, Hopkins was

Ⓐ so scared he ran away.

Ⓑ shot three times.

Ⓒ injured carrying another man off the field.

Ⓓ captured and sent to a prison camp.

3. Hopkins was captured

Ⓐ in a bear trap.

Ⓑ while he was recovering in a field hospital.

Ⓒ because he went back to pick some blackberries.

Ⓓ while he was fighting in his second battle.

4. Hopkins was sent to

Ⓐ Andersonville prison camp.

Ⓑ his hometown.

Ⓒ fight for the Southern army.

Ⓓ Georgia to recover from his wounds.

READING BETWEEN THE LINES

An *inference* is a conclusion drawn from facts. A *generalization* is a general statement, idea, or rule that is supported by facts. Analyze the story by choosing the best answer to each question below.

1. What conclusion can you draw from paragraph 5?

Ⓐ There was no food left in the entire army.

Ⓑ Corn and wheat were the main crops of the region.

Ⓒ Hopkins knew his regiment would need food.

Ⓓ Hopkins was not hungry.

2. What conclusion can you draw from paragraph 12?

Ⓐ Hopkins was still able to walk after being wounded.

Ⓑ Hopkins was not able to take part in the battle.

Ⓒ Most of the Civil War battles were fought in the summer.

Ⓓ Soldiers were required to carry officers off the field.

3. What generalization can you make from this story?

Ⓐ Almost every Union soldier was injured or captured.

Ⓑ All the heroes in the Civil War fought for the Union.

Ⓒ Some ordinary men became heroes during the Civil War.

Ⓓ No soldier can really be considered a hero.

4. What inference can you make from this story?

_____

_____

_____

_____

_____

_____

_____

_____

_____

_____

A Very UnCivil War

DETERMINING CAUSE AND EFFECT

Choose the best answers for the following questions to show the relationship between what happened in the story (*effects*) and why those things happened (*causes*).

1. **Because Charles Hopkins' family opposed slavery, Charles**

   Ⓐ left home to start his own slave trade business.

   Ⓑ knew compassion from an early age.

   Ⓒ did not want to disappoint his father.

   Ⓓ decided to join the Confederate army.

2. **What happened because Charles Hopkins wanted to serve his country?**

   Ⓐ He joined the Union army when the Civil War began.

   Ⓑ He began spying for the Union army while working on the Underground Railroad.

   Ⓒ He became a letter carrier for the Confederates.

   Ⓓ He started working in field hospitals during the Civil War.

3. **Why did their regiment think Charles Hopkins and his friends had been shot?**

   Ⓐ Hopkins told them a story about being shot at by Confederates.

   Ⓑ Their faces and clothing were stained with something that looked like blood.

   Ⓒ Hopkins was carrying two of his friends who couldn't walk.

   Ⓓ The regiment had heard shots and seen some Confederate soldiers running away.

4. **Why was Charles Hopkins hospitalized for a year and a half?**

   Ⓐ He had typhoid fever.

   Ⓑ He'd been shot in the head.

   Ⓒ The doctors were worried he'd get hurt again if they allowed him to fight.

   Ⓓ His father wouldn't allow Hopkins to come home to recover.

USING CONTEXT CLUES

Skilled readers can often find the meaning of unfamiliar words by using *context clues*. This means they study the way the words are used in the text.

Use the context clues in the excerpts below to determine the meaning of each **bold-faced** word. Then choose the answer that best matches the meaning of the word.

1. "Charles Fern Hopkins knew **compassion** from the time he was very young."

CLUE: "He grew up in a New Jersey home that was opposed to slavery."

   Ⓐ harness-making

   Ⓑ his parents

   Ⓒ sympathy

   Ⓓ slavery

2. "The men quickly realized that their **provisions** were not following them to their new camp."

CLUE: "Hopkins and his friends disobeyed orders by searching the countryside for food."

   Ⓐ supplies

   Ⓑ horses

   Ⓒ water barrels

   Ⓓ documents

3. "Hopkins and his fellow **comrades** hadn't realized that enemy soldiers had snuck inside."

CLUE: "One time Hopkins and his friends were fired upon while picking blackberries."

   Ⓐ rivals

   Ⓑ dogs

   Ⓒ companions

   Ⓓ uniforms

4. "Unfortunately, [Hopkins' decision to return to battle] had serious **consequences**."

CLUE: "By the end of the day, Hopkins was captured."

   Ⓐ truths

   Ⓑ actions

   Ⓒ illnesses

   Ⓓ results

A Very UnCivil War

A Letter from Prison

by Shirley Jordan

Mail wagons delivered letters to and from soldiers.

[1]The Civil War lasted four years. Each side took about 200,000 prisoners. One in every seven died before he could be released.

[2]Old factories and warehouses became prisons. When those were full, men were sometimes placed in stockades. These were open acres of land, fenced all around.

[3]Prisoners were expected to shelter themselves however they could. Below, a Union prisoner writes home. He's in Andersonville. That was the Confederate prison in Georgia.

June 20, 1864

My dearest Martha,

[4]*This poor excuse for a letter may never reach you. But I will take that chance. My heart is so full. I must write down what has happened these last weeks.*

[5]*On May 11, I was following General Sheridan on an attack against Richmond. A bullet caught my horse in the throat. I ran into the woods. All at once, I was surrounded by rebel soldiers.*

[6]*Three weeks have passed since they marched me here to Andersonville. It is an open space with guarded fences all around. Some say there are 30,000 men here. It is very crowded, and the prison is filthy.*

[7]*The Georgia sun beats down on us. No trees of any kind give us shade. And we have no roof over our heads unless we can find a way to build a shelter ourselves.*

[8]*Our water comes from a stream. It is no wider across than I am tall, and it is about ankle-deep. Before it reaches us, the stream passes through the guards' camp. By the time it gets here, it is dark in color. It gives off a terrible smell.*

⁹*Since we have no other water, we drink and cook from the stream. I am learning to strain, or filter, it as best I can. I found a torn piece of burlap from a prisoner who died last week. I strain the water through that.*

¹⁰*The camp cookhouse is next to the stream. That adds rotting food and grease to the already foul water. Should I wonder, dear Martha, that so many men here suffer from fever?*

¹¹*We have little shelter from the hot June sun. But we can stretch coats and scraps of blankets over ourselves. The rain cools us some. We are glad for thunderstorms. Then we wash ourselves and our clothes.*

¹²*A few men have made low mud houses from the dirty water and clay soil. An army buddy, James, had agreed to build such a hut with me. We made our plan last night. But when I awoke this morning, he lay on the ground beside me—dead. I will try to find another man to build with.*

¹³*Each evening, we are given our rations for all the next day. We get a square of corn bread. It is made with the cob ground in with the kernels.*

¹⁴*The other men have taught me to pick out the weevils. A few men just leave them in. They have come to like the taste.*

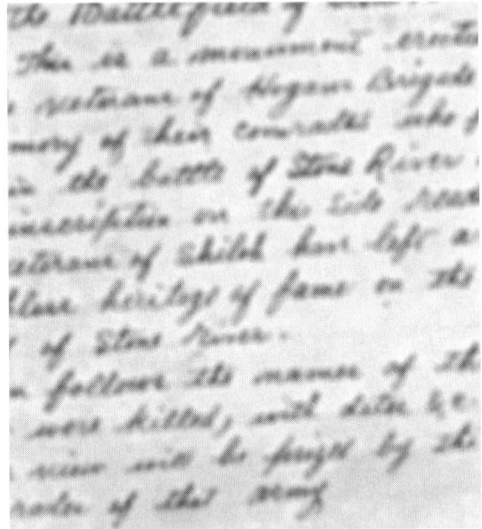

¹⁵*Some days, we have a small piece of salted pork too. About twice a week we have two tablespoons of rice. A man next to me says we receive two tablespoons of molasses each month, but I have not seen that happen.*

¹⁶*The men around me are thin as skeletons. Nearly half have no clothes at all. I think I might stay alive on the food given to me. However, the fear I have is of illness. Food will not keep me alive if it comes back up.*

¹⁷*Dozens around me stare into space or just lie about the ground. Men die here at the rate of 75 a day.*

¹⁸*We must all watch out for one another. I spend much time trying to cheer the weakest men. In the morning, each group of 90 must line*

up for roll call. If a man is missing, his group will receive no rations that day.

[19] I am sorry to bring all this sad news to you, Martha, but it helps to write this letter. Remembering our life in New York is what keeps me going.

[20] There is one sure way out of the pain and suffering here. It is one I pray I will not be driven to take.

[21] I told you there were no trees in the stockade. Here is the reason. They were cut down to make a fence out of the upright trunks. I judge it to be about 20 feet high. Near the top are small platforms. The guards sit there with their rifles.

[22] About 20 feet inside that high fence is a smaller one. It runs parallel to it. This smaller fence is known as the "dead line." You could put a foot or finger over that inside fence. But it will be blown away by a flurry of bullets from the guards.

[23] By now, dear Martha, I think you've guessed what I meant by "a way out of the misery." Just yesterday, I saw a man hobble to the inner fence. He looked to see if the guard was watching. When he knew he had been seen, he moved forward.

[24] Taking his last bit of energy, he climbed over the inner fence. In an instant, the guards filled his body with bullets. Clearly, that man wanted to escape Andersonville—in the only way he could.

[25] I promise not to do something so foolish, dear Martha. Though the days ahead may be difficult, I will do all I can to go on. I pray this war will end—and while I am still strong enough to find my way back to New York. I long to hold you and the children.

I ask your prayers.

Your loving husband,

Nathan

If you have been timing your reading speed for this story, record your time below.

_____ : _____

Minutes   **Seconds**

UNDERSTANDING THE MAIN IDEA

The following questions will demonstrate your understanding of what the story is about, or the *main idea*. Choose the best answer for each question.

1. This story is mainly about

Ⓐ the conditions in a Confederate prison.

Ⓑ how to smuggle letters from a prison.

Ⓒ an inmate who died trying to escape.

Ⓓ a wife's reaction to a letter from her imprisoned husband.

2. This story could have been titled

Ⓐ "Digging a Tunnel."

Ⓑ "The Joys of Andersonville."

Ⓒ "Misery All Around."

Ⓓ "Get Paper from Prisoner Number 92."

3. Which detail best supports the main idea of this story?

Ⓐ General Sheridan led an attack against Richmond on May 11.

Ⓑ Trees at Andersonville were cut down to make a fence.

Ⓒ The men ate corn bread.

Ⓓ Men died at Andersonville at the rate of 75 per day.

4. Find another detail that supports the main idea of this story. Write it on the lines below.

_____

_____

_____

RECALLING FACTS

The following questions will test how well you remember the facts in the story you just read. Choose the best answer for each question.

1. Nathan wrote a letter to

Ⓐ his son.

Ⓑ his commanding officer.

Ⓒ his wife.

Ⓓ the leaders of the Confederate army.

2. The men in Andersonville got water by

Ⓐ collecting snow and melting it over fires.

Ⓑ dipping it out of a filthy stream.

Ⓒ paying the guards with buttons from their uniforms.

Ⓓ writing letters to Congress and requesting it.

3. Some of the prisoners found shelter

Ⓐ between the two fence lines.

Ⓑ in the groves of oak trees inside Andersonville.

Ⓒ in mud huts they built themselves.

Ⓓ in caves they found along the hillsides.

4. Using what you learned from reading this story, draw an aerial view of Andersonville prison on another sheet of paper.

A Very UnCivil War

READING BETWEEN THE LINES

An *inference* is a conclusion drawn from facts. A *generalization* is a general statement, idea, or rule that is supported by facts. Analyze the story by choosing the best answer to each question below.

1. **What conclusion can you draw from paragraphs 5–6?**

   Ⓐ Nathan was trying to capture General Sheridan.

   Ⓑ Nathan was captured by rebel soldiers.

   Ⓒ Nathan was excited to see his friends in the woods.

   Ⓓ Nathan is the new guard at Andersonville prison.

2. **What conclusion can you draw from paragraphs 13–15?**

   Ⓐ The prisoners were given very little edible food.

   Ⓑ The prisoners were very well fed.

   Ⓒ Nathan thought the cob was the best part of the corn bread.

   Ⓓ Nathan would complain no matter what he had to eat.

3. **What generalization can you make from this story?**

   Ⓐ Many Civil War prisoners were treated poorly in prison camps.

   Ⓑ Being captured was always a welcome break from the fighting.

   Ⓒ No one left Andersonville alive.

   Ⓓ Some guards were very kind and did what they could for prisoners.

4. **It can be inferred from the story that**

   Ⓐ being taken prisoner was three times as deadly as fighting in a Civil War battle.

   Ⓑ many men died from disease, hunger, and poor conditions in Civil War prisons.

   Ⓒ it was against prison rules to write a letter to family members.

   Ⓓ no matter how bad it was, prisoners always had fresh water.

DETERMINING CAUSE AND EFFECT

Choose the best answers for the following questions to show the relationship between what happened in the story (*effects*) and why those things happened (*causes*).

1. **Because there were no trees inside the prison area,**

   (A) the men had to order their lumber from outside the prison.

   (B) there was no protection from the sun.

   (C) the water was dirty and smelly.

   (D) most of the animals had disappeared as well.

2. **What happened because the stream ran through the guards' camp?**

   (A) Guards sent secret messages to the men downstream.

   (B) The guards were ordered not to use the stream water.

   (C) The water was filthy from being used by the guards.

   (D) The camp was washed away during the spring floods.

3. **Why did Nathan need to find another building partner?**

   (A) Nathan's first partner escaped from the prison.

   (B) The guards didn't approve Nathan's first choice for a partner.

   (C) The prison rules said men had to switch partners once a week.

   (D) His original partner died before they could build a hut.

4. **Why was Nathan afraid of illness?**

   (A) He knew his body would be too weak to survive.

   (B) He was afraid to make his wife and children ill.

   (C) He had feared all kinds of sickness since childhood.

   (D) A fellow prisoner had warned Nathan what would happen if he got sick.

A Very UnCivil War

USING CONTEXT CLUES

Skilled readers can often find the meaning of unfamiliar words by using *context clues*. This means they study the way the words are used in the text.

Use the context clues in the excerpts below to determine the meaning of each **bold-faced** word. Then choose the answer that best matches the meaning of the word.

1. "When [factories and warehouses] were full, men were sometimes placed in **stockades**."

CLUE: "These were open acres of land, fenced all around."

 Ⓐ pens

 Ⓑ forts

 Ⓒ cattle barns

 Ⓓ jails

2. "No trees of any kind give [prisoners] **shade**."

CLUE: "The Georgia sun beats down on [prisoners]."

 Ⓐ hint

 Ⓑ small bit

 Ⓒ sun protection

 Ⓓ sunglasses

3. "Each evening, we are given our **rations** for all of the next day."

CLUE: "We get a square of corn bread. . . . Some days, we have a small piece of salted pork too."

 Ⓐ reasons

 Ⓑ food

 Ⓒ wages

 Ⓓ water

4. "I **long** to hold you and the children."

CLUE: "I pray this war will end—and while I am still strong enough to find my way back to New York."

 Ⓐ wide

 Ⓑ lengthy

 Ⓒ wordy

 Ⓓ want

End-of-Unit Activities

1. **The name of this unit is "Risking It All for Freedom."
   Think about each story. What was risked? Who did the
   risking? Did more than one person risk something? Fill
   out the chart below, choosing one individual from each
   story to analyze.**

	Who Made the Risk?	What Was Risked?	What Was the Outcome?
LESSON 5			
LESSON 6			
LESSON 7			
LESSON 8			

Now take a look at your chart. Which individual do you think took the biggest risk?
What was that risk? Why? Explain your answer on the lines below.

_____

_____

_____

_____

_____

_____

A Very UnCivil War

End-of-Unit Activities

2. Rank each of the stories in this unit, from the one you liked the most to the one you liked the least. For each story, write one interesting fact you learned. Then tell why you liked the story you ranked _1_ the best.

LESSON 5 Ranking _____

_____

_____

_____

_____

LESSON 6 Ranking _____

_____

_____

_____

_____

LESSON 7 Ranking _____

_____

_____

_____

_____

LESSON 8 Ranking _____

_____

_____

_____

_____

Why did you like the story you ranked _1_ the best?

_____

_____

_____

_____

Words-Per-Minute Chart

Directions:

Use the chart to find your words-per-minute reading speed. Refer to the reading time you recorded at the end of each article. Find your reading time in seconds along the left-hand side of the chart or minutes and seconds along the right-hand side of the chart. Your words-per-minute score will be listed next to the time in the column below the appropriate lesson number.

No. of Words	Lesson 5	Lesson 6	Lesson 7	Lesson 8	
	1064	1474	1085	947	
80	798	1106	814	710	1:20
100	638	884	651	568	1:40
120	532	737	543	474	2:00
140	456	632	465	406	2:20
160	399	553	407	355	2:40
180	355	491	362	316	3:00
200	319	442	326	284	3:20
220	290	402	296	258	3:40
240	266	369	271	237	4:00
260	246	340	250	219	4:20
280	228	316	233	203	4:40
300	213	295	217	189	5:00
320	200	276	203	178	5:20
340	188	260	191	167	5:40
360	177	246	181	158	6:00
380	168	233	171	150	6:20
400	160	221	163	142	6:40
420	152	211	155	135	7:00
440	145	201	148	129	7:20
460	139	192	142	124	7:40
480	133	184	136	118	8:00
500	128	177	130	114	8:20
520	123	170	125	109	8:40
540	118	164	121	105	9:00
560	114	158	116	101	9:20
580	110	152	112	98	9:40
600	106	147	109	95	10:00
620	103	143	105	92	10:20
640	100	138	102	89	10:40
660	97	134	99	86	11:00
680	94	130	96	84	11:20
700	91	126	93	81	11:40
720	89	123	90	79	12:00
740	86	120	88	77	12:20
760	84	116	86	75	12:40
780	82	113	83	73	13:00
800	80	111	81	71	13:20
820	78	108	79	69	13:40

Seconds

Minutes and Seconds

A Very UnCivil War

UNIT THREE—

in the heat of battle

Tools of War

by Shirley Jordan

[1]Many advances in the weapons and methods of war were made during the Civil War. Some were successful. Others were not. The most popular advancement came with the guns used.

[2]Both Confederate and Union soldiers used many different types of rifles. One of the most common was the Springfield rifle. It was made in Massachusetts. It weighed nine pounds, and it was nearly five feet long.

[3]To load his rifle, a soldier took out a paper-wrapped package. It held gunpowder. He also grabbed a bullet from a pouch hanging from his belt.

[4]He bit off the end of the package, and he poured powder down the barrel. Then he pushed the bullet into the barrel. He used a long metal stick. It was called a ramrod. With practice, a man could load and fire three times in a minute!

[5]In later battles, the Springfield rifle was replaced by breech-loading rifles. A soldier could load it from the side, so he could remain hidden on the ground rather than having to stand up.

[6]Most Union soldiers received breech-loading weapons, but few were given to the Confederate troops. This difference was a big advantage for the Northern army.

[7]The cannon was another common tool of war. Most Civil War cannons were old. Firing them was dangerous. When the cannon was fired, it would recoil, or jump back. Sometimes it recoiled several feet.

[8]Then men would have to roll it back into position. They'd swab out the inside and reload it.

[9]Cannons could do much damage to the enemy. So troops always tried to capture enemy cannons.

[10]Cannon barrels were made from iron or bronze. The Civil War

versions of the barrels had spiral grooves. These barrels sent shells spinning forward in a long, flat arc. These newer weapons were prized on the battlefield.

[11]Troops also used ironclad ships as tools. When the war began, Union ships closed off the whole coast of the Confederacy. This was called a blockade. They wanted to keep military supplies and food from reaching the Southern states.

[12]As the war continued, both sides built many ships. But the Confederacy never quite overcame the effects of the blockade.

[13]In 1862, Southern forces raised a large Union ship from where it had sunk. It was the *Merrimac*. They covered it with sheets of metal. This made it an ironclad ship. The Confederates made the ship their own.

[14]The *Merrimac* destroyed two of the Union's finest wooden ships— and this was in its first fight!

[15]But the U.S. government had built its own ironclad warship. It was named the *Monitor*. It was small, and it was shaped like a drum. It moved low in the water.

[16]The *Monitor* had a revolving gun holder. The ship turned easily, and the guns could change their aim in just a few seconds.

[17]On March 9, 1862, the two ships met in battle. They fought for five hours. Both suffered damage.

[18]Finally, the *Merrimac* sailed away. It sent one last shot over the top of the *Monitor*.

[19]No one has ever decided who won the battle that day. Most call it a tie.

[20]The Civil War was the first time that soldiers used dugouts and trenches. These are simply holes dug in the ground. They gave soldiers some protection during battle.

[21]Black men volunteered to fight for the Union. At first, they were not allowed guns. Instead they often dug trenches for the white soldiers.

These officers, shown on her deck, served on the original Monitor.

[22]If a soldier could crawl into a trench, he might be protected from a hand grenade. This was a chemical hand bomb. It had been tested a few times in other wars.

[23]Grenades helped defeat the Confederacy at Vicksburg in 1863.

[24]Some battles took thousands of lives. Each army lost about 25 out of every 100 men in a battle. At Gettysburg, the number was as high as 80 out of 100!

[25]A soldier wanted to be sure his family knew of his fate, so he was likely to write his name and address on a handkerchief or piece of paper. Then he pinned it to his uniform before going into battle.

[26]The use of military dog tags, or metal identification necklaces, is now common. Sometimes soldiers are badly wounded and can't answer questions about themselves. So dog tags contain the basic information.

[27]The Confederacy had trouble moving the mail. Jefferson Davis remembered his "camel project." He'd conducted it for President Franklin Pierce in 1853. He had used camels to transport supplies to the West. He knew there were still trained camels they could use.

[28]So he sent some cowboys to round up the animals.

[29]From 1863 to 1865, a few camels were used to move the Confederate mail. Most of this was done in the western states. The animals were hard to train, and the noise of war bothered them. So they became hard to handle.

[30]After the war, the federal government sold the animals to circuses. Some were turned loose in the desert. Some of those were hunted by the Apache Indians.

[31]Other camels disappeared into the hills. Even in the 1900s, their offspring were sometimes seen in California's Death Valley.

If you have been timing your reading speed for this story, record your time below.

_____ : _____

Minutes   *Seconds*

UNDERSTANDING THE MAIN IDEA

The following questions will demonstrate your understanding of what the story is about, or the *main idea*. Choose the best answer for each question.

1. This story is mainly about

Ⓐ the hammers, wrenches, and shovels used in warfare.

Ⓑ what Civil War officers learned from previous wars.

Ⓒ how the Confederacy moved mail during the Civil War.

Ⓓ the different aids Civil War armies used.

2. This story could have been titled

Ⓐ "Civil War Weapons and Methods."

Ⓑ "Stubborn Camels."

Ⓒ "The Mail Must Go Through!"

Ⓓ "Hand Me That Hammer, Joe."

3. Which detail best supports the main idea of this story?

Ⓐ The cannon was a very destructive tool of war.

Ⓑ When the war began, Union ships closed off the whole coast of the Confederacy.

Ⓒ Black men fought for the Union.

Ⓓ The battle between the *Merrimac* and the *Monitor* was considered a tie.

4. Find another detail that supports the main idea of this story. Write it on the lines below.

_____

_____

_____

RECALLING FACTS

The following questions will test how well you remember the facts in the story you just read. Choose the best answer for each question.

1. Civil War soldiers loaded their guns with

Ⓐ rags from old uniforms.

Ⓑ acorns from trees.

Ⓒ gunpowder and bullets.

Ⓓ poison-tipped darts.

2. The Springfield rifle was later replaced by the

Ⓐ breech-loading rifle.

Ⓑ bronze cannon.

Ⓒ grenade.

Ⓓ Massachussetts shotgun.

3. A soldier facing battle wrote his name

Ⓐ in the battle ledger.

Ⓑ on a paper pinned to his uniform.

Ⓒ to prove he could write well enough to serve in the army.

Ⓓ in the ashes of the campfire.

4. The Confederates used camels to

Ⓐ cross the sandy battlefields.

Ⓑ pull their cannons.

Ⓒ confuse the Union soldiers, who used horses.

Ⓓ carry mail.

—————■—————

READING BETWEEN THE LINES

An *inference* is a conclusion drawn from facts. A *generalization* is a general statement, idea, or rule that is supported by facts. Analyze the story by choosing the best answer to each question below.

1. **What conclusion can you draw from paragraph 21?**

   Ⓐ Black men did not fight for the South.

   Ⓑ Black men wanted to serve the Union.

   Ⓒ Black men did not know how to shoot rifles.

   Ⓓ White soldiers couldn't dig trenches.

2. **What conclusion can you draw from paragraphs 27–29?**

   Ⓐ The camels had been turned loose in the West.

   Ⓑ The camels had been sent back to Asia.

   Ⓒ Camels were easy to train.

   Ⓓ The best way to send mail was to hire a camel and driver.

3. **What generalization can you make from this story?**

   Ⓐ None of the soldiers liked the new methods of war.

   Ⓑ War can bring about improvements in weapons and tools.

   Ⓒ All the weapons used during the Civil War were new.

   Ⓓ Most soldiers used outdated methods and weapons during the Civil War.

4. **It can be inferred from the story that**

   Ⓐ loading a rifle was an easy task to learn.

   Ⓑ no one had ever thought of covering a ship with sheets of metal before.

   Ⓒ soldiers had to reload guns and cannons each time they fired.

   Ⓓ dogs were useful in identifying soldiers wounded on the battlefield.

A Very UnCivil War

DETERMINING CAUSE AND EFFECT

Choose the best answers for the following questions to show the relationship between what happened in the story (*effects*) and why those things happened (*causes*).

1. Because soldiers didn't like to stand up to load their rifles,

Ⓐ the generals had to hire boys to load the rifles.

Ⓑ a new gun that could be loaded from the side was invented.

Ⓒ many soldiers used their empty guns as clubs during battle.

Ⓓ the grenade became a popular weapon.

2. What happened because cannons would roll back when fired?

Ⓐ The soldiers had to roll them back into place after every shot.

Ⓑ A young soldier invented blocks to put behind the wheels.

Ⓒ The front lines of battling armies often spread farther and farther apart.

Ⓓ Several soldiers were hurt when they got caught behind the cannons.

3. Why were the camels hard to handle?

Ⓐ Most Confederate soldiers were too short to get on the camels' backs.

Ⓑ The camels were scared of the noise of war.

Ⓒ The camels couldn't hear what their riders were telling them to do.

Ⓓ The camels didn't like to carry mail.

4. On the lines below, write the effect for the following cause in the story.

CAUSE: Soldiers wanted their families to know if they were wounded or killed in battle.

_____

_____

_____

_____

_____

_____

_____

_____

————▆————

USING CONTEXT CLUES

Skilled readers can often find the meaning of unfamiliar words by using *context clues*. This means they study the way the words are used in the text.

Use the context clues in the excerpts below to determine the meaning of each **bold-faced** word. Then choose the answer that best matches the meaning of the word.

1. "This difference was a big **advantage** for the Northern army."

CLUE: "A soldier could load [a breech-loading rifle] from the side, so he could remain hidden on the ground rather than having to stand up. . . . Most Union soldiers received breech-loading weapons, but few were given to the Confederate troops."

Ⓐ benefit

Ⓑ loss

Ⓒ annoyance

Ⓓ part

2. "When the cannon was **fired**, it would recoil, or jump back."

CLUE: "[The men would] swab out the inside and reload it."

Ⓐ heated

Ⓑ burned

Ⓒ let go

Ⓓ shot

3. "Troops also used **ironclad** ships as tools."

CLUE: "[The Confederates] covered [a ship] with sheets of metal."

Ⓐ wooden

Ⓑ strong

Ⓒ metal-covered

Ⓓ cloth-covered

4. "The *Monitor* had a **revolving** gun holder."

CLUE: ". . . the guns could change their aim in just a few seconds."

Ⓐ fixed

Ⓑ movable

Ⓒ circular

Ⓓ square

A Very UnCivil War

The Family That Couldn't Escape

by Shirley Jordan

Manassas was the site of the Bull Run battles.

[1] Wilmer McLean had had enough. Union soldiers in blue uniforms were marching from the North. Confederate troops in gray were coming from the South. His Manassas, Virginia, farm was right between the two groups.

[2] McLean wanted his family to be safe. But how could he keep them from harm?

[3] In town, nobody thought the Civil War would happen. Americans would never fight other Americans!

[4] Well, the news about Fort Sumter was a worry, and President Lincoln had called for men to join the army. But would there be a war? McLean and his friends didn't want to believe it. Couldn't this problem about slavery be settled some other way?

[5] It was the spring of 1861. Seven Southern states had already left the Union. The farmers in those states were angry. They were afraid that President Lincoln would make them free their slaves.

[6] How could they be expected to plant large pieces of land alone? How could a man grow cotton, tobacco, and sugar without many workers? These things couldn't be done without slaves. The landowners decided to fight to keep things the way they were!

[7] McLean was a Southerner, and Virginia was a slave state. He knew how the planters felt. If it came to a fight, he would surely have to side with his neighbors.

[8] Because McLean lived so far north in Virginia, his home was only 20 miles from Washington, D.C. If fighting came, his farm would be right in the middle of the battle.

[9] Now it looked as if both North and South wanted to control the

railroad line in Manassas. Each day, war seemed closer.

[10]More Union forces gathered at Manassas. The railroad line helped move troops and supplies.

[11]Confederate soldiers marched to McLean's farm too. The two armies camped on either side of a winding stream called Bull Run.

[12]For weeks, no shots were fired. Sticky summer heat brought mosquitoes and flies. The insects got into everything. The food was poor. Both armies lived on dried meat and hard bread.

[13]The men slept on bare dirt. When it rained, mud covered the tired soldiers and their weapons.

[14]An outbreak of measles swept through the camps. Even without a war, many soldiers died each week.

[15]Wilmer McLean invited the Confederate officers to move into his farmhouse. The officers asked for a signal tower, and he allowed one to be built in his front yard. He would do all he could to help.

[16]Still, McLean worried about his family's safety.

[17]The rich people of nearby Washington, D.C., didn't worry at all. "A battle down at Manassas would end the war," they said.

[18]The first shots rang out on July 21, 1861.

[19]The people of Washington dressed for an outing. They piled their children into family wagons. Then they added baskets of food. They added some blankets to sit on. They rode 20 miles down the road to Manassas.

[20]"This is just like a picnic," some said. "How exciting! A chance to see a real battle!"

[21]But what happened wasn't a game. The Confederate army rushed forward. They forced the Union soldiers backward, toward Washington.

[22]Many soldiers were wounded. As bloody bodies filled the road, the picnic crowd panicked. They rushed back to the city in terror.

[23]The battle shocked Wilmer McLean too. A large cannon shell burst through his kitchen window. And before the fighting stopped, wounded Confederate soldiers filled his house. Instead of a headquarters, his house had turned into a hospital.

[24]McLean was glad that the South had won that day. But his heart was heavy as he looked around him. His home was damaged. His fields were trampled. His fences were down. All

his crops had been torn up or destroyed.

[25]No one in his own family was hurt, but McLean knew how close the danger had come. He gathered his loved ones at the end of the day.

[26]"This will not happen again," he said firmly. "I promise you. I will take you far from here to the Virginia hill country. We will start over there. The war will never reach us."

[27]And he kept his promise. He found a small village. It was more than a hundred miles south of Manassas. It was far from the railroad line. No army would have reason to come there.

[28]The McLeans built a two-story brick house. It had a wide porch and a fine set of front steps.

[29]From the porch, the family could see the town square and the brick tavern. A new courthouse stood nearby. Because of that, the village was named Appomattox Court House.

[30]The Civil War lasted for four more years. But McLean felt safe for most of that time.

The McLeans built a second home in Appomattox County.

[31] Then in 1865, the Union troops won battle after battle. They pushed the Confederate soldiers farther into the South.

[32] Again, the McLeans could hear the sounds of war. The family gathered.

[33] McLean said, "We must pray the fighting won't find us again."

[34] On April 9, 1865, a tired Confederate colonel came down the street. He looked around. Then he climbed the stairs to the McLeans' wide porch.

[35] The colonel had a question. You see, General Robert E. Lee and the Confederates were ready to give up. There would be no more war. No more blood would flow.

[36] But Lee needed a place to surrender, or give up the fight. He and the Union General Ulysses S. Grant had to work out the peace plans.

[37] The colonel asked, "Would you allow your parlor to be used for the meeting?"

[38] Wilmer McLean was glad to see an end to the fighting. So he agreed. After all, it had all begun in his kitchen in Manassas. Shouldn't it end in his new home?

If you have been timing your reading speed for this story, record your time below.

_____ : _____

Minutes   **Seconds**

UNDERSTANDING THE MAIN IDEA

The following questions will demonstrate your understanding of what the story is about, or the *main idea*. Choose the best answer for each question.

1. This story is mainly about

Ⓐ a slave family that tried to escape a plantation.

Ⓑ one family's experience during the Civil War.

Ⓒ a family trapped in a snowstorm near Washington, D.C.

Ⓓ a group of Confederate soldiers captured by the Union.

2. This story could have been titled

Ⓐ "The Underground Railroad."

Ⓑ "We Need Our Slaves!"

Ⓒ "Coming Full Circle."

Ⓓ "The South Secedes from the Union."

3. Which detail best supports the main idea of this story?

Ⓐ In town, no one thought the Civil War would happen.

Ⓑ The landowners decided to fight to keep things the way they were.

Ⓒ Both North and South wanted to control the railroad line.

Ⓓ The fighting began in McLean's kitchen in Manassas.

4. Find another detail that supports the main idea of this story. Write it on the lines below.

_____

_____

_____

RECALLING FACTS

The following questions will test how well you remember the facts in the story you just read. Choose the best answer for each question.

1. Southern landowners were afraid that President Lincoln would

Ⓐ make them fight for the Union.

Ⓑ take away their land.

Ⓒ force them to free their slaves.

Ⓓ send them to prison.

2. If it came to war, Wilmer McLean would

Ⓐ side with the South.

Ⓑ join the Union army.

Ⓒ take his family to Europe.

Ⓓ free his slaves.

3. Wilmer McLean moved his family

Ⓐ into Washington, D.C.

Ⓑ so they'd be able to help the Confederate soldiers.

Ⓒ to a place where no battles would be fought.

Ⓓ after the Confederate army burned his house down.

4. On another sheet of paper, draw a picture of the meeting between Wilmer McLean and the tired colonel who asked to use his parlor. In a caption, write what you think McLean might have said after the colonel made his request.

———■———

An *inference* is a conclusion drawn from facts. A *generalization* is a general statement, idea, or rule that is supported by facts. Analyze the story by choosing the best answer to each question below.

1. What conclusion can you draw from paragraphs 11–12?

Ⓐ The armies didn't have any ammunition for their rifles.

Ⓑ Local farmers kept the armies supplied with fresh food.

Ⓒ The armies weren't fighting each other yet.

Ⓓ Mosquitoes are a common problem in Virginia.

2. What conclusion can you draw from paragraphs 19–20?

Ⓐ Civilians thought watching a battle would be fun.

Ⓑ It took several days to reach Manassas from Washington, D.C.

Ⓒ The people expected to see a long, drawn-out battle.

Ⓓ The families expected it to be cold in Manassas.

3. What generalization can you make from this story?

Ⓐ Everybody was so excited about the Civil War, they didn't worry about their safety.

Ⓑ Some innocent people were in danger during Civil War battles.

Ⓒ The Confederate army made sure all local people left before a battle.

Ⓓ All Civil War battles lasted for several days.

4. It can be inferred from the story that

Ⓐ a Civil War battle could destroy everything a farmer owned.

Ⓑ battles were advertised in newspapers so people could come and watch.

Ⓒ the South won the Civil War.

Ⓓ the Civil War only lasted a few months.

———— ■ ————

DETERMINING CAUSE AND EFFECT

Choose the best answers for the following questions to show the relationship between what happened in the story (*effects*) and why those things happened (*causes*).

1. **Because Wilmer McLean lived close to Washington, D.C., and a railroad,**

   Ⓐ the Confederate army asked him to move his family.

   Ⓑ he was sure no battles would take place near his home.

   Ⓒ President Lincoln used his house as a headquarters.

   Ⓓ he was worried that the fighting would harm his family.

2. **What happened because an outbreak of measles swept through the army camps?**

   Ⓐ There was very little food.

   Ⓑ The armies didn't shoot at each other.

   Ⓒ Many soldiers died even though there was no war.

   Ⓓ McLean invited the Confederate officers to live in his house.

3. **Why did Wilmer McLean move his family to the hill country?**

   Ⓐ He'd always heard how beautiful it was there.

   Ⓑ It was close to the coast, in case they needed to leave the country.

   Ⓒ He thought there was little chance battles would be fought nearby.

   Ⓓ A railroad ran directly through his land.

4. **Why did the Confederate colonel ask to use Wilmer McLean's parlor?**

   Ⓐ The colonel needed to rest after so many battles.

   Ⓑ General Lee needed a place to meet with General Grant.

   Ⓒ The colonel wanted to hold a victory party in the parlor.

   Ⓓ President Lincoln was coming to town for tea.

USING CONTEXT CLUES

Skilled readers can often find the meaning of unfamiliar words by using *context clues*. This means they study the way the words are used in the text.

Use the context clues in the excerpts below to determine the meaning of each **bold-faced** word. Then choose the answer that best matches the meaning of the word.

1. "An **outbreak** of measles swept through the camps."

CLUE: "Even without a war, many soldiers died each week."

Ⓐ argument
Ⓑ broom
Ⓒ riot
Ⓓ epidemic

2. "The people of Washington dressed for an **outing**."

CLUE: ". . . they added baskets of food. They added some blankets to sit on."

Ⓐ picnic
Ⓑ sailing
Ⓒ battle
Ⓓ storm

3. "As bloody bodies filled the road, the . . . crowd **panicked**."

CLUE: "They rushed back to the city in terror."

Ⓐ ate quickly
Ⓑ flew upright
Ⓒ was alarmed
Ⓓ celebrated

4. "But Lee needed a place to **surrender**."

CLUE: "[Lee] and the Union General Ulysses S. Grant had to work out the peace plans."

Ⓐ host a party
Ⓑ give up
Ⓒ sleep
Ⓓ camp

A Very UnCivil War

The Battle of Gettysburg

by Shirley Jordan

On July 1, 1863, John Burns heard the sound of gunfire. It was nearby.

[2] The 72-year-old Pennsylvania shoemaker hurried to his front porch. Union soldiers were rushing past the house. They seemed ready for battle. They were headed west toward the McPherson farm.

[3] John Burns went inside. With a grim smile, he took down his old musket.

[4] "They won't turn me down a third time," he vowed. "They said I was too old to enlist in 1861. They said the same thing in '62."

[5] The aging Scotsman ran a hand through his white hair. He rested his musket on his shoulder.

[6] "Gettysburg is my town, and I'm going to fight for it."

[7] A three-day struggle followed. It has been called the greatest battle ever fought on American soil.

[8] Burns followed the Union soldiers. He hurried down the road and walked past Gettysburg's Lutheran Seminary. The sound of gunfire grew louder.

[9] He soon came upon a line of men in blue. They were soldiers of the 150th Pennsylvania Volunteers.

[10] The surprised men welcomed him with smiles. No one asked his age. The soldiers talked Burns into trading his old musket for a newer weapon.

[11] Burns watched as the men filled their pockets with bullets. Then he did the same.

[12] "Those rebels will divide our country," he said. "They'll learn their lesson—right here at Gettysburg."

[13] Quickly, Burns pushed his way to the front line. His eyes gleaming, he fired away. Years of hunting had given him a sharp aim. He did as well as the younger men around him.

[14] Early that afternoon, Burns received his first wound. He stopped long enough to have it bandaged.

[15] Now the Union forces were being driven back. They needed him. So Burns went to the front line again. This time, he joined a trained army unit. It was called the Iron Brigade.

[16] He received two more flesh wounds. Then a call to withdraw, or retreat, ended his fighting for that day.

[17] That evening, the Union troops retreated through the streets of Gettysburg. Many men were captured by the Confederate forces.

[18] General Meade was the commander of the Union forces. He gathered his remaining men on Cemetery Hill. This was south of town. Earlier in the day, the men had fought among the tombstones there.

[19] The first day at Gettysburg was a tragic one. The Union had 12,000 dead and wounded. The Confederacy had 8,000.

[20] That night, cries of the wounded filled the air. Union soldiers with bullet wounds staggered through town. They were thirsty and in pain.

[21] Gettysburg citizens crept out of their homes with pitchers of water. Many families took men in. Others set up hospitals in the town's churches and warehouses.

[22] Local and military doctors were kept busy removing bullets. They were often forced to cut off an arm or leg.

[23] The Confederate forces took over Gettysburg on July 2. But John Burns was not arrested, for he was not a Union soldier.

[24] Not one of Gettysburg's citizens was harmed by the Confederates. The 2,400 townspeople stayed in their houses. They were afraid of what might happen next.

[25] Many families took food and bedding into their cellars. This offered at least some protection from the bullets and cannonballs.

[26] Confederate officers knocked on doors. They ordered the people of Gettysburg to take in wounded rebel soldiers. Some houses were filled with bleeding men from both sides.

[27] Mothers soon learned that these young men were much like their own sons. Some women told neighbors about how strange dinnertime had been that second night. At their tables might have been three or four injured Union soldiers. They'd be eating alongside three or four Confederate soldiers.

[28] All were weak with pain. So there was no fighting. As one

Nearly 50,000 Union and Confederate soldiers were killed or wounded during the battle of Gettysburg.

Gettysburg mother put it, "It could have been a family reunion. And these boys might have been cousins."

[29]By July 3, additional troops had come to the aid of General Meade's forces. This larger army began to drive the Confederates back.

[30]At one point, 12,000 Southern troops tried to break through the Union line. In that battle—Pickett's Charge—the Northern troops held firm. More than 5,000 young men died there. All died in just one hour.

[31]The Southern forces could no longer continue the battle. On the morning of July 4, General Lee withdrew his men into Virginia.

[32]The two armies finally marched away from Gettysburg. They left behind a town in ruins.

[33]Many homes had more than 100 bullet holes in them. Some had been burned. Nearly 50,000 killed and wounded soldiers were left behind. Men who needed care were crowded into every building

in town. There were only a few doctors.

[34]The men and women of Gettysburg went to work. They found papers on many bodies. These papers told each soldier's hometown.

[35]Women and girls wrote letters to the soldiers' families. John Burns and the other men and boys buried hundreds of dead horses. The terrible smell of death was everywhere.

[36]Pennsylvania's governor was Andrew Curtin. He set aside a large piece of land for a cemetery. Within four months, all the dead were buried, and the graves were properly marked.

[37]On November 19, 1863, the new cemetery was dedicated. The main speaker was Edward Everett. He gave a two-hour talk.

[38]Next came President Lincoln. He said only 270 words. His speech is known as the Gettysburg Address.

[39]His speech lasted three minutes. But the power of his words will remain with Americans forever.

If you have been timing your reading speed for this story, record your time below.

_____ : _____

Minutes   Seconds

A Very UnCivil War

UNDERSTANDING THE MAIN IDEA

The following questions will demonstrate your understanding of what the story is about, or the *main idea*. Choose the best answer for each question.

1. This story is mainly about

Ⓐ older Civil War soldiers.

Ⓑ the type of weapons used in the Battle of Gettysburg.

Ⓒ the largest battle fought during the Civil War.

Ⓓ a famous cemetery for Civil War soldiers.

2. This story could have been titled

Ⓐ "Fighting for Your Town."

Ⓑ "The Innocent Victims."

Ⓒ "The Forty-Mile Walk."

Ⓓ "The Greatest Battle."

3. Which detail best supports the main idea of this story?

Ⓐ The 72-year-old Pennsylvania shoemaker hurried to his front porch.

Ⓑ The Battle of Gettysburg has been called the greatest battle ever fought on American soil.

Ⓒ General Meade was the commander of the Union forces.

Ⓓ Lincoln's speech became known as the Gettysburg Address.

4. Find another detail that supports the main idea of this story. Write it on the lines below.

_____

_____

_____

RECALLING FACTS

The following questions will test how well you remember the facts in the story you just read. Choose the best answer for each question.

1. The Battle of Gettysburg lasted

Ⓐ three days.

Ⓑ three hours.

Ⓒ two days.

Ⓓ two weeks.

2. At the end of the first day of the Battle of Gettysburg,

Ⓐ the Confederates were retreating.

Ⓑ the Union forces were retreating.

Ⓒ only a few soldiers had died.

Ⓓ a large party was held in the streets.

3. Confederate officers ordered Gettysburg citizens to

Ⓐ give them all their food to feed the soldiers.

Ⓑ leave the town.

Ⓒ burn their houses.

Ⓓ take in wounded rebel soldiers.

4. After the battle, Pennsylvania's governer

Ⓐ joined the Confederacy.

Ⓑ set aside land for a new cemetery.

Ⓒ ordered the residents to rebuild the town.

Ⓓ asked the armies to pay for the damage they caused.

READING BETWEEN THE LINES

An *inference* is a conclusion drawn from facts. A *generalization* is a general statement, idea, or rule that is supported by facts. Analyze the story by choosing the best answer to each question below.

1. What conclusion can you draw from paragraphs 13–14?

Ⓐ Burns was afraid to fight in the war.

Ⓑ Burns was opposed to hunting.

Ⓒ Burns was anxious to fight.

Ⓓ Burns stopped fighting after one day.

2. What conclusion can you draw from paragraphs 26–27?

Ⓐ There were many fights over the Gettysburg dinner tables.

Ⓑ The Gettysburg women were excellent cooks.

Ⓒ Dinnertime was later that evening because of the fighting.

Ⓓ The soldiers were willing to eat with their enemies.

3. What generalization can you make from this story?

Ⓐ Some older men were not allowed to enlist in the Union army.

Ⓑ The Union army would allow anyone with a gun to fight.

Ⓒ Most Union soldiers were very young men.

Ⓓ The Union army only allowed men over 60 to enlist.

4. It can be inferred from the story that

Ⓐ not very many Americans have heard of the Gettysburg Address.

Ⓑ President Lincoln was not a very good speaker.

Ⓒ Lincoln's address at Gettysburg has become a famous speech.

Ⓓ there were five speakers at the dedication of the Gettysburg cemetery.

A Very UnCivil War

DETERMINING CAUSE AND EFFECT

Choose the best answers for the following questions to show the relationship between what happened in the story (*effects*) and why those things happened (*causes*).

1. **Because John Burns heard a battle near his home, he**

    Ⓐ packed a bag and rode his horse to his brother's house.

    Ⓑ decided to join the fight on the side of the Union.

    Ⓒ hid in the cellar and waited for the battle to end.

    Ⓓ started collecting bandages and water for the wounded.

2. **What happened because John Burns had hunted for years?**

    Ⓐ He had an old rifle.

    Ⓑ He was not nervous about being in a battle.

    Ⓒ He had shot at several kinds of animals.

    Ⓓ He had very good aim with his rifle.

3. **Why did John Burns return to the front line after being wounded?**

    Ⓐ He thought the Union needed him.

    Ⓑ His officers told him to go to the front line.

    Ⓒ He wanted to save one of his new soldier friends.

    Ⓓ He wanted to die.

4. **Why did the Gettysburg citizens bring water into the streets?**

    Ⓐ They wanted to clean the streets.

    Ⓑ The wounded soldiers were thirsty.

    Ⓒ The soldiers' horses needed to drink some water.

    Ⓓ The Union army was buying water from residents.

USING CONTEXT CLUES

Skilled readers can often find the meaning of unfamiliar words by using *context clues*. This means they study the way the words are used in the text.

Use the context clues in the excerpts below to determine the meaning of each **bold-faced** word. Then choose the answer that best matches the meaning of the word.

1. "[Burns said,] 'They said I was too old to **enlist** in 1861.' "

CLUE: " '[The Union] won't turn me down a third time,' [Burns] vowed."

   Ⓐ join the army

   Ⓑ go to school

   Ⓒ learn to read

   Ⓓ walk a long distance

2. "A three-day **struggle** followed."

CLUE: "It has been called the greatest battle ever fought on American soil."

   Ⓐ night

   Ⓑ celebration

   Ⓒ fight

   Ⓓ storm

3. "The first day at Gettysburg was a **tragic** one."

CLUE: "The Union had 12,000 dead and wounded. The Confederacy had 8,000."

   Ⓐ easy

   Ⓑ terrible

   Ⓒ happy

   Ⓓ short

4. "On November 19, 1863, the new cemetery was **dedicated**." (paragraph 37)

Write what you think the bolded word means. Then record the context clues that led you to this definition.

Meaning:

_____

_____

_____

Context Clues:

_____

_____

_____

The Brave Drummer Boy

by Peg Hall

There are many sad facts about the War Between the States. One of the saddest is that both the Union and Confederate armies were full of young boys. Some soldiers were barely old enough to be away from home.

2 This is the story of one such boy. His name was Johnny Clem. Johnny was a drummer boy for the 22nd Michigan, a regiment of the Union army.

3 Johnny was hard at work fixing the strap on his drum, so he hardly noticed when Sergeant Warren came into the tent.

4 "You should be in bed, Johnny," said the sergeant.

5 Johnny looked up and smiled at his friend. "You sound like my mother," he said. "It's not that late."

6 "Maybe not. But you're only ten years old, even if you are a Union soldier. And I think tomorrow will be a big day, so you need to rest."

7 "Do you mean that we'll fight tomorrow?" asked Johnny. "The battle's been going on for two days already and they haven't called our regiment in yet."

8 "They'll need us soon enough," answered Sergeant Warren. "So go on, Johnny. Get to bed. If Rosey catches you, we'll both be in trouble."

9 Johnny laughed at that. "Rosey" was General Rosecrans. He had a habit of slipping around the camp at night. If he heard any of his soldiers talking, he would rap on the tent walls with his sword. That was a warning to settle down and go to sleep.

10 Johnny knew the general cared about his soldiers. And in return, the men loved General Rosecrans. In fact, the 22nd Michigan was like a

family—especially to Johnny, since he had no family of his own.

[11]Johnny sighed and put down his drum. "I just wish I could have a gun," he said.

[12]The sergeant frowned. He had heard this complaint from Johnny before. If he had his way, the boy would never carry a gun. Johnny might be old enough to be a drummer boy, but he was much too young to carry a gun.

[13]Then the sound of a bugle rang out. The sad notes of taps signaled the end of another day. Soon lights were out and campfires were dead.

It was quiet and still all through the camp. Everyone wanted a good night's sleep before the next day's battle.

[14]But in the morning it was the sound of guns that woke Johnny and the sergeant. The fighting seemed closer.

[15]"I think the battle is moving to the west," Sergeant Warren said. "That means we're losing. They'll have to call in our regiment now, Johnny. If that happens, promise me you'll take care of yourself."

[16]Just then an officer walked through the camp. He called out,

Union soldiers drilled with the drummer in the lead.

A Very UnCivil War

"Get ready to march, men!"

[17]Quickly, the men of the 22nd lined up. Johnny set his hat straight on his head. He picked up his drum and walked to the front of the line.

[18]Johnny began to beat his drum, and the men started forward. The sun shone down on them as they marched through the green fields. It was hard to believe that a terrible battle was going on only a few miles away.

[19]But there was a battle. And before long Johnny's regiment was in the thick of it. Shots rang out from Confederate soldiers to their left. The Union soldiers answered with shots of their own.

[20]Then there was a flash in the sky. "Down!" shouted Sergeant Warren.

[21]Johnny dropped with the others. A cannon shell passed over their heads.

[22]Once again Johnny wished for a gun. It isn't fair, he thought. The Confederates can shoot at me, but I can't shoot back.

[23]Soon the men were up and marching again. Every time they saw the flash of a cannon, they dropped to the ground.

[24]At last the line of soldiers turned off the road. They could hear the sounds of battle just ahead. And they could see a hill—Horseshoe Ridge, it was called. Dust rose into the air as Confederate soldiers ran across the dry ground along the top of the ridge.

[25]A Union soldier on horseback rode up to Johnny. He carried a flag in one hand. "Here, boy," the soldier said, "you be our marker today." He passed the flag to Johnny.

[26]Pride filled Johnny's heart. As marker, it was his job to plant the flag and show where the Confederate soldiers were heading. It was an important job.

[27]"We're going to charge the ridge," said Sergeant Warren. "Get ready, Johnny. And remember what I said about being careful."

[28]Then the order came. "Charge!"

[29]The brave soldiers ran up the hill with their guns held before them. Most of them had never been in battle before. Still, they moved forward, dodging bullets. Johnny ran along with them. He carried the Union flag in his hands.

[30]As the troops reached the top of the hill, the Confederates fell back. The Union soldiers gave a cheer. The rebels were giving up the hill!

[31]But it wasn't for long. The Confederates came forward again.

Now it was the Union soldiers who fell back.

[32]It was then that General Steedman rode up. He took the flag from Johnny. Then he shouted, "Go back, boys! Go back! But our flag won't go with you!"

[33]The general's words made the Union soldiers remember who they were. They were the men of the 22nd Michigan. And they weren't going to let the Confederates win this battle.

[34]So, with the general in the lead, the men pushed ahead. Johnny followed them. Bullets rained down upon them, and some men fell. The general's horse was shot out from under him. But that didn't stop General Steedman. He went ahead on foot, still carrying the flag.

[35]Eventually the men of the 22nd Michigan caught up with General Steedman. Johnny caught up too. The general ran over to Johnny and handed him the flag. "They're on the run, boy!" he shouted. "Mark the spot."

[36]Johnny held the flag high and watched the Confederate soldiers. Soon he could see which way they were going. He ran to the spot and planted the flag. The Union soldiers headed toward it on the trail of the rebels.

[37]Johnny turned and saw General Steedman leading his men. He was on a new horse.

[38]At last the Union army reached the top of the hill. Horseshoe Ridge was theirs! The Confederates kept shooting, but they couldn't take the ridge back.

[39]Johnny sat down to rest. Beside him lay a young soldier who had been killed in the battle. And next to the soldier was a gun.

[40]Johnny dropped his drum. What good was it in battle? Who could even hear it over the noise?

[41]He picked up the gun. Then he looked through the dead soldier's things and found some bullets.

[42]The gun felt good in Johnny's hands. His father had taught him to shoot. In fact, Johnny was a crack shot. He could hit a squirrel at a hundred yards.

[43]Johnny began to shoot at the men in gray. He saw some men fall. But he wasn't sure his shots had hit them. He kept on shooting, hardly seeing what was going on around him.

[44]More Confederate soldiers had come to join the others. Now the rebels stormed the hill. The Union army began to fall back. At last General Rosecrans decided it was

foolish to try to hold the hill.

[45]By late afternoon only three regiments were left on Horseshoe Ridge. One of them was the 22nd Michigan—Johnny among them.

[46]Suddenly Johnny realized that there were men in gray all around him. He loaded his gun and kept on shooting.

[47]A Confederate officer rode toward Johnny. He was going as fast as the wind. And in his hand he held a sword.

[48]Johnny stood his ground as the horse came closer. The officer's sword was shining in the sunlight.

[49]But Johnny didn't even look at the sword. He looked carefully though the sight of the gun. Just as the sword swung toward him, Johnny fired. The bullet went straight through the officer's heart. The man fell from his horse.

[50]All afternoon the men of the 22nd Michigan kept fighting. They shot until they ran out of bullets. Then they used their unloaded guns as clubs.

[51]But none of them was any braver than Johnny. The ten-year-old drummer boy had killed a Confederate officer. His bullets had killed others as well.

[52]Several days after the battle Johnny was called to play the drum. There was to be a parade, he was told. General Rosecrans and General Steedman would both be there.

[53]Johnny was drumming away when he heard his name.

[54]"Sergeant John Clem, step forward," said a voice. It was General Steedman.

[55]Johnny looked toward the general. "But I'm not a sergeant," he said.

[56]"You are now," said the general. "I've heard of your bravery in battle. Step up now and get your sergeant's stripes."

[57]So that night Johnny sewed the stripes of a sergeant to his coat. And from then on he was a soldier of the 22nd Michigan.

If you have been timing your reading speed for this story, record your time below.

_____ : _____

Minutes   **Seconds**

UNDERSTANDING THE MAIN IDEA

The following questions will demonstrate your understanding of what the story is about, or the *main idea*. Choose the best answer for each question.

1. This story is mainly about

Ⓐ a boy who drummed for the Confederate army.

Ⓑ a boy who fought bravely in a battle.

Ⓒ learning the different drum rolls for a battle.

Ⓓ a drummer boy who saved the life of the flag carrier.

2. This story could have been titled

Ⓐ "Follow the Drum."

Ⓑ "My Friend the Sergeant."

Ⓒ "The Noise of Battle."

Ⓓ "Johnny Gets a Gun."

3. Which detail best supports the main idea of this story?

Ⓐ The sergeant told Johnny Clem to go to bed.

Ⓑ If the general heard any of his soldiers talking, he would rap on the tent walls with his sword.

Ⓒ Johnny began to beat his drum, and the men started forward.

Ⓓ Just as the Confederate's sword swung toward him, Johnny fired.

4. Find another detail that supports the main idea of this story. Write it on the lines below.

_____

_____

_____

RECALLING FACTS

The following questions will test how well you remember the facts in the story you just read. Choose the best answer for each question.

1. Johnny Clem was a young

Ⓐ drummer for the Union army.

Ⓑ drummer for the Confederate army.

Ⓒ escort for President Lincoln.

Ⓓ scout for General Rosecrans.

2. Johnny Clem really wanted to

Ⓐ be a drummer his whole army career.

Ⓑ fight in a battle.

Ⓒ carry the flag for his regiment.

Ⓓ go home to his family.

3. A Union soldier asked Johnny Clem to

Ⓐ bring him a new horse after the one he was riding got shot.

Ⓑ take a message to Sergeant Warren.

Ⓒ keep his hands up as the soldier captured Johnny.

Ⓓ carry the regiment's flag.

4. Johnny Clem got a gun from

Ⓐ Sergeant Warren as a birthday gift.

Ⓑ the Sears-Roebuck catalog.

Ⓒ a dead soldier.

Ⓓ his special hiding place in a tree.

A Very UnCivil War

An *inference* is a conclusion drawn from facts. A *generalization* is a general statement, idea, or rule that is supported by facts. Analyze the story by choosing the best answer to each question below.

1. What conclusion can you draw from paragraph 1?

Ⓐ The Union and Confederate armies wanted only young boys to fight.

Ⓑ The Union and Confederate armies allowed young boys to join.

Ⓒ The Union and Confederate armies made sure young boys wrote home regularly.

Ⓓ The Union and Confederate armies turned away anyone younger than 16.

2. What conclusion can you draw from paragraphs 53–56?

Ⓐ Johnny was promoted to a sergeant for his bravery at Horseshoe Ridge.

Ⓑ General Steedman had asked Johnny if he wanted to be a sergeant.

Ⓒ Johnny refused to be a drummer boy for the parade.

Ⓓ Johnny and the general were very good friends.

3. Write a generalization about Civil War soldiers that can be made after reading this story.

_____

_____

_____

_____

_____

_____

_____

_____

_____

4. It can be inferred from the story that

Ⓐ Johnny died in battle.

Ⓑ the battle at Horseshoe Ridge was the last battle of the war.

Ⓒ there were many brave soldiers in the battle at Horseshoe Ridge.

Ⓓ Johnny was the only person fighting the Confederates at Horseshoe Ridge.

DETERMINING CAUSE AND EFFECT

Choose the best answers for the following questions to show the relationship between what happened in the story (*effects*) and why those things happened (*causes*).

1. **Because General Rosencrans and his men cared about one another,**

   Ⓐ they were crying when they went into battle.

   Ⓑ Johnny felt as if they were a family.

   Ⓒ they stayed up late many nights talking and laughing.

   Ⓓ no wounded man was ever left on the battlefield.

2. **What happened because Johnny Clem complained that he didn't have a gun?**

   Ⓐ Sergeant Warren bought him a gun for his birthday.

   Ⓑ Sergeant Warren suggested Johnny send for his gun from home.

   Ⓒ Sergeant Warren frowned at the thought of a ten-year-old with a gun.

   Ⓓ Sergeant Warren asked General Rosencrans if Johnny could fight the next day.

3. **Why did Johnny's regiment get called into battle?**

   Ⓐ They were the best at fighting in the hills.

   Ⓑ All the other regiments had been sent home.

   Ⓒ President Lincoln ordered them to take Horseshoe Ridge.

   Ⓓ The Union was losing and needed more men.

4. **Why did General Steedman say the regiment's flag wasn't going with the men?**

   Ⓐ No one could find Johnny, who was carrying the flag.

   Ⓑ The general wanted to inspire the men to fight harder.

   Ⓒ The flag was being sent to the wife of the dead flag carrier.

   Ⓓ They already had too much to carry without worrying about the flag.

USING CONTEXT CLUES

Skilled readers can often find the meaning of unfamiliar words by using *context clues*. This means they study the way the words are used in the text.

Use the context clues in the excerpts below to determine the meaning of the **bold-faced** words. Then choose the answer that best matches the meaning of the word.

1. "The sad notes of **taps** signaled the end of another day."

CLUE: "Then the sound of a bugle rang out. . . . Soon lights were out and campfires were dead."

    Ⓐ a bugle call to go to bed

    Ⓑ a drum roll to march

    Ⓒ a bugle call to wake up

    Ⓓ a drum roll to hide

2. "Dust rose into the air as Confederate soldiers ran across the dry ground along the top of the **ridge**."

CLUE: "And [Johnny's regiment] could see a hill—Horseshoe Ridge, it was called."

    Ⓐ sharp edge

    Ⓑ hilltop

    Ⓒ corner

    Ⓓ bump

3. " 'Here, boy,' the soldier said, 'you be our **marker** today.' "

CLUE: "[The soldier] passed the flag to Johnny."

    Ⓐ monument

    Ⓑ artist's pen

    Ⓒ drummer

    Ⓓ flag bearer

4. "Johnny was a **crack** shot."

CLUE: "He could hit a squirrel at a hundred yards."

    Ⓐ loud

    Ⓑ excellent

    Ⓒ poor

    Ⓓ gap

End-of-Unit Activities

1. **What adjectives can you think of to describe the Civil War? Fill in the web below. Use words to describe the Civil War. Then record a quote or fact from one of the stories in this unit to back up each adjective you choose.**

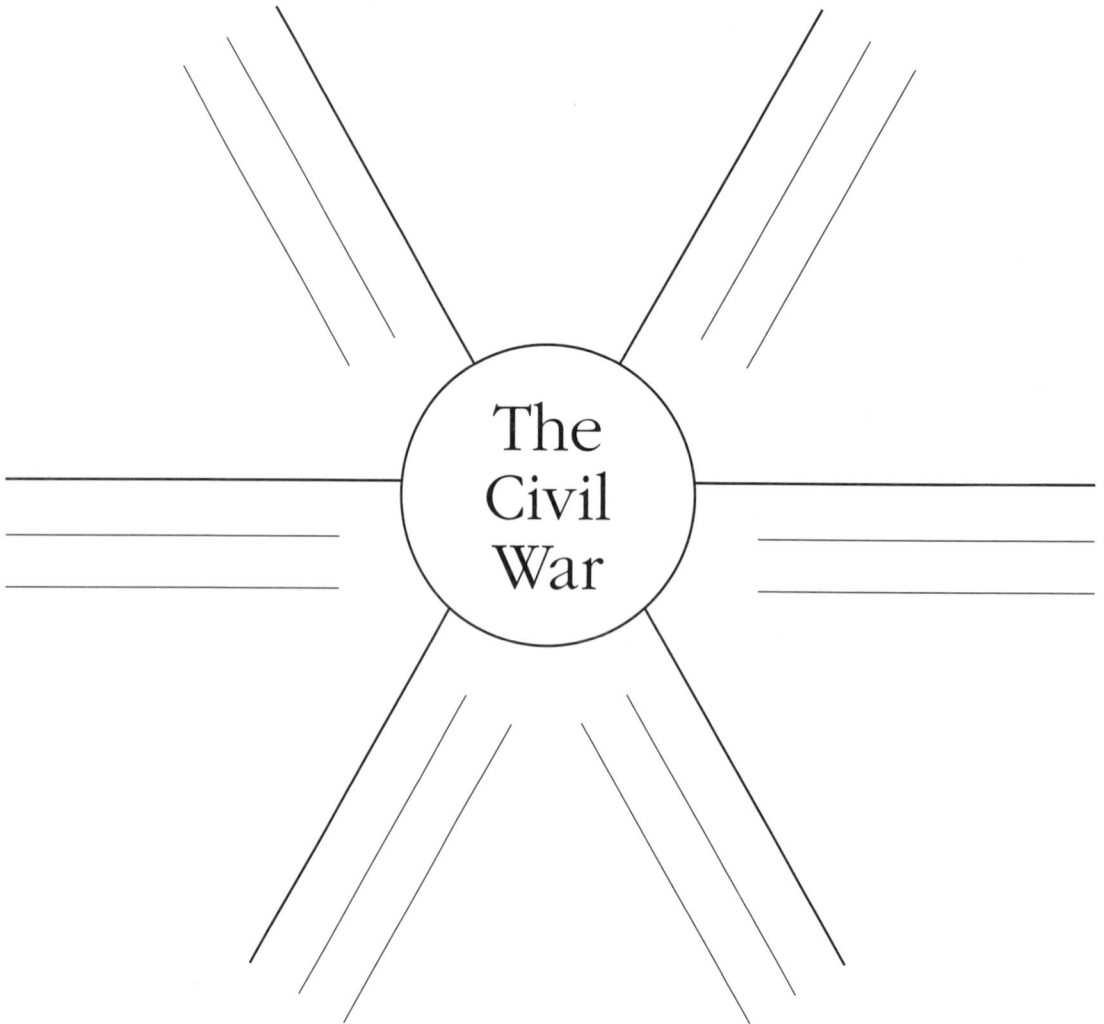

The Civil War

A Very UnCivil War

End-of-Unit Activities

2. **Rank each of the stories in this unit, from the one you liked the most to the one you liked the least. For each story, write one interesting fact you learned. Then tell why you liked the story you ranked *1* the best.**

LESSON 9 Ranking _____

_____

_____

_____

_____

LESSON 10 Ranking _____

_____

_____

_____

_____

LESSON 11 Ranking _____

_____

_____

_____

_____

LESSON 12 Ranking _____

_____

_____

_____

_____

Why did you like the story you ranked *1* the best?

_____

_____

_____

_____

Words-Per-Minute Chart

Directions:

Use the chart to find your words-per-minute reading speed. Refer to the reading time you recorded at the end of each article. Find your reading time in seconds along the left-hand side of the chart or minutes and seconds along the right-hand side of the chart. Your words-per-minute score will be listed next to the time in the column below the appropriate lesson number.

	Lesson 9	Lesson 10	Lesson 11	Lesson 12	
No. of Words	**858**	**951**	**922**	**1518**	
80	644	713	692	1139	**1:20**
100	515	571	553	911	**1:40**
120	429	476	461	759	**2:00**
140	368	408	395	651	**2:20**
160	322	357	346	569	**2:40**
180	286	317	307	506	**3:00**
200	257	285	277	455	**3:20**
220	234	259	251	414	**3:40**
240	215	238	231	380	**4:00**
260	198	219	213	350	**4:20**
280	184	204	198	325	**4:40**
300	172	190	184	304	**5:00**
320	161	178	173	285	**5:20**
340	151	168	163	268	**5:40**
360	143	159	154	253	**6:00**
380	135	150	146	240	**6:20**
400	129	143	138	228	**6:40**
420	123	136	132	217	**7:00**
440	117	130	126	207	**7:20**
460	112	124	120	198	**7:40**
480	107	119	115	190	**8:00**
500	103	114	111	182	**8:20**
520	99	110	106	175	**8:40**
540	95	106	102	169	**9:00**
560	92	102	99	163	**9:20**
580	89	98	95	157	**9:40**
600	86	95	92	152	**10:00**
620	83	92	89	147	**10:20**
640	80	89	86	142	**10:40**
660	78	86	84	138	**11:00**
680	76	84	81	134	**11:20**
700	74	82	79	130	**11:40**
720	72	79	77	127	**12:00**
740	70	77	75	123	**12:20**
760	68	75	73	120	**12:40**
780	66	73	71	117	**13:00**
800	64	71	69	114	**13:20**
820	63	70	67	111	**13:40**
840	61	68	66	108	**14:00**

Seconds

Minutes and Seconds

A Very UnCivil War